T5-AGA-666

The Supreme Court in Modern Role

James Stokes Lectureship on Politics

New York University–Stokes Foundation

The Supreme Court in Modern Role

The Supreme Court in Modern Role

by Carl Brent Swisher

New York University Press
Washington Square, 1958

Library of Congress catalogue card number: 58-5041
Manufactured in the United States of America

Preface

The Supreme Court of the United States stands at the converging point of our public law, national politics, and public policy. Sooner or later the major problems of our national life find their way in some form to the magnificent marble edifice in Washington that bears above its portal the promise of "equal protection under law." The problems vary from period to period. Because of both their variation and their intensity, the work of the Court, viewed over the more than century and a half of its history, looks like a series of intermittent crises, crises that have had to be faced in the judicial search for the ideal of stability and clarity in constitutional and statute law. As we move farther and farther from the time and the conditions of the drafting of the Constitution, the Supreme Court must rely increasingly on its estimate of the dominant and settled sentiments of current times rather than on history or textual exegesis for its source of constitutional meaning. As a result, the difficulty of interpretation increases rather than decreases with the passing years.

The current major problems of the nation, and hence also of the Supreme Court, involve questions of both the scope of the positive powers of government and the definition of constitutional limitations. These problems occur not so much in connection with the scope of property rights, as in earlier years, as with the rights of persons and groups of persons in relation to the law. The Court in its modern role has had to deal in critical circumstances with problems of subversion, with the changing place of the military in our traditionally civilian culture, and with problems of race as extensions of conflicts generated long ago. These areas of judicial activity are discussed herein, with the purpose of illuminating the essential nature of the judicial process in the operations of this high tribunal.

The occasion of this analysis was the preparation of lectures for delivery at New York University under the auspices of the James Stokes Lectureship on Politics. As in the writing of most books, obligations have been incurred to many persons, including Dean Harold Stoke and Professor Marshall Dimock and others at New York University who have been responsible for administration of the lectureship. Students at Johns Hopkins University have aided greatly in the development of ideas and the formulation of subject matter. Miss Shirley Thomas, a graduate student and a junior instructor in constitution law, has done extensive work on the text of the lectures and, together with Mrs. Edna L. Fulton, has typed a draft for delivery and publication. Part of Chapter V underwent some modification as a result of helpful criticisms from friends who heard it delivered as a presidential address before an annual meeting of the Southern Political Science Association. Appreciation is expressed to the *Journal of Politics,* the official organ of that association, for permission to re-present the materials here. Acknowledgment is also made for permission from Columbia University Press and Harvard University Press, respectively, to quote from Benjamin N. Cardozo, Jr., *Paradoxes of Legal Sciences* and Charles Fairman, *Mr. Justice Miller and the Supreme Court.*

CARL BRENT SWISHER

September, 1957

Contents

The Supreme Court in Modern Role

I *The Court and the Sweep of History*

In a book entitled *The Struggle for Judicial Supremacy,* which was published in 1941, Attorney General Robert H. Jackson talked about a constitutional renaissance that had begun with Supreme Court opinions handed down in 1937, a renaissance that had been in the nature of a rediscovery of the Constitution itself. Prior to that renaissance, Jackson contended, "Constitutional law had become, not the law of the Constitution, but the law *about* the Constitution." Now, by contrast, we were back to the original sweep and vigor of the clauses that conferred power on the federal government, and the interpretation of restrictive clauses had been deflated to approximate the original meaning.[1]

The sense of victory here expressed by the highest law officer of the federal government, who was soon himself to become a member of the Supreme Court, was typical of the reactions of New Deal liberals everywhere. As he further put the matter, and as was widely felt, "my generation has won its fight to make its own impression on the Court's constitutional doctrine." [2] A revolution or a renaissance had taken place, and the people had come into their own.

The events referred to by the Attorney General wrought tremendous changes in the American constitutional pattern, but the sequence of changes by no means stopped with the course of these events. Partly because of the clashing attitudes of new justices but also because of national and world-wide disturbing events during the ensuing two decades, unforeseen transformations continued to take place. This book will deal with the changing pattern of judicial restraints upon government, the relation of law to the threat of subversion, the constitutional place of the military, the legal resolution of race conflict, and, speaking broadly, the position of the Supreme Court in the government of the United States today.

For background, however, we need to look at the historical pattern of Supreme Court activity, including not merely the constitutional renaissance of the 1930's and early 1940's but also the earlier developments and transitions that in their own time seemed to mark crises equal to those in our current experience. Attorney General Jackson and other New Dealers wrote and talked as if the period of their immediate past had been the only important period of alleged and long-range deviation from the Constitution, and seemed to believe that their own corrective action would leave the Supreme Court and the Constitution once more in stable status. Critics of the New Deal, on the other hand, treated New Deal action as constitutional heresy without precedent and seemed to assume that prior to this disturbance the course of constitutional development had been relatively smooth. The assumptions on both sides represent fictions for the convenience of the authors. Throughout our history, periods of relative and uneasily maintained stability in constitutional law have alternated with more or less abrupt changes. Both the changes and the stability have been conditioned in part by men on the Supreme Court, and by the sweep of events beyond the range of judicial control but which nevertheless had constitutional impact. The summary of familiar constitutional history to be presented hereafter will call to mind occasions on which the presence on the Supreme Court of particular personnel was all-important in determining the stability or the changes in legal patterns. It will call to mind also the grinding pressures put upon stability-seeking judges by the course of events within our democracy.

1 Of the nature of the judicial task when a court operates under great social pressures and when circumstances are changing so rapidly that precedents are not immediately relevant, Justice Cardozo wrote as follows:

> Diligence and memory and normal powers of reasoning may suffice to guide us truly in those fields where the judicial function is imitative or static, where known rules are to be applied to combinations of facts identical with present patterns, or, at worst, but slightly different. The travail comes when the judicial function is dynamic or creative. The rule must be announced for a novel situation where competitive analogies supply a hint or clew, but where precedents are lacking with authoritative commands.[3]

Under circumstances "where precedents are lacking with authoritative commands," the judge may strike out on his own in search of solutions in the spirit of the law. But the spirit is seldom easy to discover where the letter is unclear, and on vital issues there are many to dispute the judge's spiritual interpretation. Judges being human in their desire for community approval, it is not surprising that some of them drift with the sentiments of the times and fill the interstices of the law somewhat as if they were the direct agents of democracy. But it is also not surprising that some of them feel obligated to save society from itself where it seems to them inclined to go wrong, and fill in the blank passages with rulings to ensure what they regard as basically right even though such rightness may be unpopular. It is similarly natural that the appointment of new judges should reflect the sentiments of dominant interests at the time of appointments, and that new judges should be "liberal" in their inclinations to free society from the dead hand of the past. Such factors have been involved in most of or all the crises that have attended the unfolding of our Constitution.

Throughout its entire history, and not merely during the New Deal period, the Supreme Court has been in search of the Constitution as the judges sitting were able to see and define the Constitution, and throughout its entire history the Court has been seeking to determine the character and dimensions of its own role in the government. With respect to the Constitution generally, the formal tasks have involved determination of the scope of the power that the Constitution confers on the federal government, the line to be drawn between legislative, executive, and judicial powers, the scope of the restrictions specifically laid on governments whether federal or state, and the extent to which the existence of federal powers imposes limitations on the powers of the states, even where no such limitations are specifically prescribed. Behind the formal legal questions here involved have lain questions about the extent of the paternalistic responsibility of government at any level for the welfare of the people, the rightful allocation of such responsibility to large or small units, the degree of sanctity of rights of property, and the scope of the personal and civil rights to be sheltered within the governmental domain. Judicial attitudes on these subjects have differed tremendously from period to period and among the many judges who have sat on the high Court. Throughout its entire history, to repeat, the Supreme Court has been engaged in a search to determine the scope and the limitations of the Constitution, with many important questions never settled but subject to re-examination by changing personnel under changing circumstances.

A central task has been that of determining the scope of the Court's own power. In some periods and situations the Court has appeared to laymen so cautious and so eager to avoid decision of constitutional questions as to be derelict in the performance of its duties. At other times it has stirred popular wrath and damaged its prestige by deciding questions beyond the scope of seeming necessity. On occasion it has drawn even from its own members warnings such as that of Justice Stone in *United States v. Butler* that "Courts are not the only agency of government that must be assumed to have the capacity to govern," [4] and that for courts "the only check upon our own exercise of power is our own sense of self-restraint." [5] To this we have the counterstatement of Justice Sutherland:

> The suggestion that the only check upon the exercise of the judicial power, when properly invoked, to declare a constitutional right superior to an unconstitutional statute is the judge's own faculty of self-restraint, is both ill considered and mischievous. Self-restraint belongs in the domain of will and not of judgment. The check upon the judge is that imposed by his oath of office, by the Constitution and by his own conscientious and informed convictions; and since he has the duty to make up his own mind and adjudge accordingly, it is hard to see how there could be any other restraint.[6]

In its relations with the other branches of the federal government the Supreme Court has sometimes been most deferential and self-abnegating in the exercise of its jurisdiction. Shortly after the Civil War it refused to permit the filing of a bill to enjoin the President from enforcing the Reconstruction Acts, saying:

> Suppose the bill filed and the injunction prayed for allowed. If the President refuse obedience, it is needless to observe that the Court is without power to enforce its process. If, on the other hand, the President complies with the order of the Court and refuses to execute the acts of Congress, is it not clear that a collision may occur between the Executive and Legislative departments of the government? May not the House of Representatives impeach the President for such refusal? And in that case

> could this Court interfere in behalf of the President, thus endangered by compliance with its mandate, and restrain by injunction the Senate of the United States from sitting as a court of impeachment? [7]

The Court refused to hand down a decision that would invite such a stalemate. Yet with an adroitness that avoided official conflict John Marshall had in 1803 decided a case in such a way as to accuse the Jefferson administration of dereliction of duty, asserting piously that "It is emphatically the province and duty of the judicial department to say what the law is." [8] Later in his term Marshall handed down a decision known to be unpopular with President Jackson, to whom was attributed the perhaps apocryphal, but nevertheless characteristic, angry remark, "Well, John Marshall has made his decision, now let him enforce it." [9] The Court of the 1930's so sweepingly opposed the New Deal program as to lead to the famous Court-packing effort of that period.

2 So varied, indeed, have been the positions of the Supreme Court from the time of its first meeting in 1790 until today with respect to the powers and restraints implied in the Constitution, and the scope of its own responsibility, that the discussion in later chapters of current areas of unsettlement needs to be put in the perspective of our judicial origins and of the major transitions in constitutional interpretation. We know, of course, that the federal judicial system was expected to function in the tradition of judicial performance that had developed in England and had been followed in the colonies in America. Of the origins of the English courts we have but limited knowledge. In his *Commentaries on the Laws of England,* Sir William Blackstone had this to say about relations between judges and the king:

> It is probable, and almost certain, that in very early times, before our Constitution arrived at its full perfection, our kings in person often heard and determined causes between party and party. But at present, by the long and uniform usage of many ages, our kings have delegated their whole judicial power to

the judges of their several courts; which are the grand depositaries of the fundamental laws of the kingdom, and have gained a known and stated jurisdiction, regulated by certain and established rules, which the crown cannot now alter but by act of Parliament.[10]

We know that centuries were required for the attainment of judicial independence from the crown. We know also that the English Parliament, which we think of today primarily in terms of the legislative process, was long thought of as a kind of court which only in part made new law, or not so much made new law as found and gave statement to law that as to principle, as to the "laws of nature," was already there.[11] But the tendency in England was to isolate the judicial function more and more in the judiciary, and in the American colonies to separate legislative, executive, and judicial functions one from the others. The federal judiciary, omitted from the governmental structure provided by the Articles of Confederation, was established under the Constitution in the light of this tradition.

In the debate on the federal judiciary in the Virginia ratifying convention, a critic, William Grayson, asserted concerning the proposed Supreme Court that "This Court has more power than any court under Heaven." [12] For more than a decade the Court organized in New York in 1790 showed little likelihood of exercising any such power. Important cases were few and far between. In these cases the justices for the most part wrote seriatim opinions, which in their diversity of reasoning and expression obscured the unanimity implicit in the decisions, with resulting loss of strength to the Court as one organic body. The three men who during the decade served as Chief Justice, or at any rate those two who served more than a few months, were better equipped as politicians than as judges, and while serving as head of the Court each of the two rendered more notable service through other branches of the government than through the judiciary. The justices complained about the requirement—which but for a brief period beginning near the close of the John Adams administration lasted for more than a century—that they ride circuit to handle work in the circuit courts as well as in the Supreme Court. It was partly in resentment against this requirement that John Jay, the first Chief Justice, resigned in 1795 to become governor of the state of New York. When in 1800 President Adams asked him to return to his former judicial position he refused to do so, showing even at that date no conception of the position the Supreme Court was to occupy in the federal system. Efforts repeatedly made, he said, to put the judicial department on a proper footing had proved fruitless.

> I left the bench perfectly convinced that under a system so defective it would not obtain the energy, weight, and dignity which are essential to its affording due support to the national government, nor acquire the public confidence and respect which, as the last resort of the justice of the nation, it should possess. Hence I am induced to doubt both the propriety and the expediency of my returning to the bench under the present system. . . .[13]

3 The first great transition in the history of the Supreme Court came with the appointment of John Marshall to the position John Jay had rejected. The Court came into its own during the years between 1801 and 1835 when Chief Justice Marshall gave it prestige and direction, operating during most of those years under the conditions Jay had found intolerable. Yet there was a difference, even though a difference that Jay ought to have been able to foresee. The Marshall appointment, coinciding as it did with the succession of Jeffersonian Republicans to power in the other two branches of the federal government, came as the judiciary was left as the remaining stronghold of federalism. We do not here need to discuss the question whether, as contended by William W. Crosskey, "the period of John Marshall's Chief Justiceship was a period of constitutional decay."[14] Within the realm of such figures of speech, growth and health and decay are matters of opinion turning on the desires of writers or of the people written about. Certain it is that before the adoption of the

Constitution there were men who desired a more highly centralized government than did their fellows, and who, once the Constitution was adopted in its broad general language and largely without definition of its terms, sought to make it mean as nearly as possible what they wanted it to mean. From the point of view of these people even the federalism of John Marshall may have seemed a watered-down product and might well be referred to as "constitutional decay."

But given the frame of mind of the people in the early nineteenth century, the available alternative was not one of a stronger central government than that envisaged by the Marshall Court. It was the alternative of a weaker central government, with greater emphasis on the prerogatives of the states. The Marshall Court did not, as some might have wished, define for us a unitary government with the states reduced virtually to the level of administrative units. The political situation would not have permitted such definition even if Marshall himself or the Court as a whole had desired it. What he did do, as far as the arrival of cases before the Court permitted, was to outline a pattern of federal-state relationships in which federal authority was implemented by the doctrine of implied powers, while state powers were strictly subordinated. He ran threads of consistency through the mass of significant opinions by resorting to the device of the "opinion of the Court" instead of calling for seriatim opinions, by himself speaking for the Court in a large proportion of the important cases, and by setting an example in most instances of yielding to the opinions of his brethren where he could not win their agreement; indeed, he sometimes even delivered the opinion of the Court in such cases.[15] As a result of Marshall's strategy the opinions written by the justices came to stand virtually as a body of constitutional law, and not merely as a collection of diverse opinions on the issues in question.

The very process of phrase-making and organization of legal materials added to the weight and persuasiveness of Marshall's opinions as statements of law. Marshall's capacities in this field, developed during his practice as a lawyer, were described as follows by William Wirt, one of his distinguished contemporaries at the bar:

> This extraordinary man, without the aid of fancy, without the advantages of person, voice, attitude, gesture, or any of the ornaments of the orator, deserves to be considered as one of the most eloquent men in the world; if eloquence may be said to consist in the power of seizing the attention with irresistible force, and never permitting it to elude the grasp, until the hearer has received the conviction which the speaker contends.[16]

Marshall, Wirt continued, had the faculty of detecting at a single glance the very point on which every controversy depended. Furthermore,

> In a bad cause, his art consisted in laying his premises so remotely from the point directly in debate, or else in terms so general and specious, that the hearer, seeing no consequence which could be drawn from them, was just as willing to admit them as not; but, his premises once admitted, the demonstration, however distant, followed as certainly, as cogently, as inevitably as any demonstration in Euclid.[17]

Marshall carried these capacities over into his work as Chief Justice. He used them both in winning the support of his brethren for the positions he took in the several cases and in writing the judicial opinions that for approving readers gave Supreme Court opinions of his period their high status as statements of constitutional law.

From the point of view of future generations, an outstanding achievement was the determination in *Marbury v. Madison* that the Supreme Court had the power to strike down acts of Congress on grounds of unconstitutionality, his conviction, previously quoted, being that in instances of alleged conflict between statutes and the Constitution "It is emphatically the province and duty of the judicial department to say what the law is."[18] But for all the anger and resentment aroused among Jeffersonians about the way Marshall shaped his opinion to portray the administration as derelict in its duty, the issue of judicial review of acts of Congress was not of first importance during the Marshall period. True, the decision clinched a question of judicial power at a point where opponents of judicial power would have liked to restrict it, but after 1803 there were almost no major conflicts over the constitutionality of acts of Congress until long after the close of the Marshall regime, and no act of Congress was held unconstitutional thereafter for more than half a century.

Rather, the Marshall Court made its contemporary imprint largely through decisions that curbed not acts of Congress but the power of the states, usually with respect to rights of property. Particularly in cases involving the contract clause of the Constitution, Marshall used the power of the Court to shield property against state legislation, in all probability giving the contract clause restrictive power well beyond that intended by the framers.[19] He brought the charters of private corporations into the invulnerable position of private contracts and thereby speeded the development of such corporations as major instruments of business enterprise.[20] Only in his determination to strike down state bankruptcy laws applicable to future contracts did Marshall fail to carry the Court with him in interpretations in the contract-bankruptcy field, and there, in *Ogden v. Saunders,*[21] he wrote his only dissenting opinion on a constitutional issue.

Marshall's Court curbed the expanding claims of some state judiciaries by asserting against them the power of the Supreme Court to redetermine cases decided by state courts where questions of rights under the federal Constitution were involved,[22] thereby adding to the storm of criticism directed at the Supreme Court by the exponents of state rights. Declaring that "the power to tax involves the power to destroy," [23] it denied to a state the power to tax a branch of the federally chartered Bank of the United States. It found that bank a constitutional instrument of the federal government in a strategic statement of the doctrine of implied powers lodged in Congress. It struck down a state monopoly of steamboat navigation on navigable waters, stressing the broad scope of commerce power conferred upon Congress.[24] It protected the money power of the federal government by striking down as bills of credit a state's loan certificates that were issued to circulate as money.[25]

In these and other cases the Supreme Court curbed the outreaching powers of the states, saving room for the exercise of such power as the federal government might see fit to exercise and, since broad exercise of power by the federal government was in general not then contemplated, providing for a regime largely of laissez faire. Yet the pressures of state and parochial interests continued to mount. Property interests provoked jealousy and met attack not only on grounds of frustrated rivalry but on genuinely humanitarian grounds as well—as in the instance of the state bankruptcy case mentioned above, where, in the absence of a federal bankruptcy statute, the only relief to be had from the pressure of debt must be provided by the states.

However, a series of cases pending before the Court during Marshall's later years challenged his nationalist and laissez-faire leanings. One of them involved the claims of a highly prosperous bridge monopoly in Boston that collected tolls from people crossing the Charles River and fought against the construction of a competing bridge recently chartered by the state. Another involved the question of the constitutionality of note issues by state banks to circulate as money, at a time when expansion of the circulatory medium was greatly needed, in the face of a constitutional provision that forbade the states themselves directly to provide such note issues. Another dealt with the power of states to require shipmasters to make full reports on passengers brought in from other ports, without reference to the fact that interstate or foreign commerce might be involved.

These three cases were pending as Western democracy was coming to power in the federal government with new ideas and attitudes toward big property and big government. It was at the time of a slave rebellion in Virginia of the kind always feared by Southern masters, a rebellion in some sense in harmony with abolitionist sentiments in the North, and which aroused in Southerners the determination to curb the power of the federal government, possibly tainted with abolitionist attitudes, and to strengthen the powers of the states. It was at the time when Marshall himself was growing old and when the persuasive power of his personality and his ideas over new members of the Court was beginning to wane. In short, it was time for one of the many relatively sharp transitions that have taken place in the judicial development of our constitutional law.

4 The story of that transition is well known to history. The Court was incompletely manned at the time of the first argument of the cases outlined above, and they had to be held over for reargument. Marshall died before the Court could be restored to full membership, and when in 1837 the rearguments finally took place the Court had a new Chief Justice, Roger B. Taney, and four of the other six justices were also Jackson appointees. All three cases were decided in a vein very different from that of the Marshall Court. The Taney Court upheld the power of Massachusetts to authorize construction of a bridge that would compete with the monopoly bridge, refusing to hold, as Daniel Webster had argued, that a corporation charter should be interpreted broadly after the fashion of interpreting constitutions and that monopoly rights should be inferred even if not clearly stated. Very different from Marshall's language were such phrases as "the object and end of all government is to promote the happiness and prosperity of the community by which it is established," [26] and "While the rights of private property are sacredly guarded, we must not forget that the community also have rights, and that the happiness and well being of every citizen depends on their faithful preservation." [27] Justice Story, who thought like Marshall on constitutional issues, wrote in dissent that the opinion he had formed after the first argument of the case remained his "firm and unhesitating conviction." [28]

The Taney Court also upheld the power of a state to charter a bank to issue notes that might circulate as money even though a state might not issue such notes directly. Justice

Story dissented, asserting that a majority of the Court who had heard the first argument of the case had been of a different opinion. "Among that majority," he proclaimed solemnly, "was the late Mr. Chief Justice Marshall—a name never to be pronounced without reverence." [29] He closed with the statement that he had expressed his dissent because the public had a right to know the opinion and the reasoning of every dissenting judge—a position very different from that of Marshall when the Marshall-Story approach to constitutional law was dominant with the Court. Story added:

> I have another and strong motive—my profound reverence and affection for the dead. Mr. Chief Justice Marshall is not here to speak for himself, and knowing full well the grounds of his opinion, in which I concurred, that this act is unconstitutional, I have felt an earnest desire to vindicate his memory from the imputation of rashness, or want of deep reflection.[30]

The Taney Court held that the New York statute requiring masters of ships to give detailed reports on persons brought in from other ports was a legitimate exercise of the state's police power and did not conflict with the power of Congress to regulate interstate and foreign commerce. Justice Story again dissented, concluding with the statement:

> In this opinion I have the consolation to know that I had the entire concurrence, upon the same grounds, of that great constitutional jurist, the late Mr. Chief Justice Marshall. Having heard the former arguments, his deliberate opinion was that the act of New York was unconstitutional. . . .[31]

Although he achieved a measure of respect for Chief Justice Taney, Story continued until his own death in 1845 to bemoan the passing of the great Marshall and the old order of things on the Court. Daniel Webster and others of the Federalist-Whig stamp had similar things to say, Webster lamenting in 1847 that the present Supreme Court was no court for constitutional questions and that it wanted a strong and leading mind.[32] Yet a leading Democratic journal described Taney as follows:

> The present Chief Justice escapes from irrelevant matter with as much ease as Judge Marshall or the most distinguished of the English Judges. Like them he seizes the true question in the case, and never loses sight of it for a single instant. He strips off, gently but firmly, all the disguises with which forensic eloquence so often veils the truth, and without fear or hesitation follows wherever she may lead. . . . We are forced to . . . feel, while listening to him, that we are receiving lessons of wisdom from one, the directness and simplicity of whose mind disdain the foppery and tinsel of the rhetorician, and who uses words not as baubles to gain the admiration of a moment, but as the vehicle of useful and constructive thought.[33]

The differences between the work of the Taney Court and that of the Marshall Court were not alone or even primarily the differences between the two Chief Justices. Taney, it is true, lacked some of the persuasive power of his predecessor, and Taney's colleagues were probably less subject to persuasion by the head of the Court than were Marshall's colleagues. But beyond all that was the influence of the tides of sentiment mentioned above. The issues of regional differences were strong enough to prevent exercise of sweeping governmental power from Washington; yet there were problems of welfare that had to be solved, and therefore had to be solved at the state or local level. While the representatives of what was to become big business in future generations sought not regulation but protection and public franchises and, beyond that, laissez faire, there was a growing popular demand for government protection against irresponsible business that preyed on the public in their own interest. For the individual seekers after protection, the existence of the federal Constitution was not to be permitted to interfere with the exercise of local power. These diverse interests among the people were reflected in the diversity of Supreme Court opinions about the scope and exclusiveness of the federal commerce power, the scope of the police powers of the states, and the nature and extent of federal jurisdiction over slavery.

In spite of the differences between the Taney Court and the Marshall Court, and in spite of the diversity of opinion in important cases, the Court had gained or regained such prestige by the mid-1850's that some members and some politicians believed that a formal decision of the Court with respect to the power of Congress over slavery in the territories might settle that stormy issue. The decision in the Dred Scott case demonstrated the tragic mistake of unnecessary judicial intervention in political controversies on which the people were fundamentally divided. The decision became an issue in national politics and the prestige of the Court dropped to an all-time low—in those states, at any rate, that remained loyal to the Union. Through the war period the Court presented a sad picture of an institution functioning as part of the government but suspected of disloyalty. In support of that interpretation we now know that the Chief Justice saw the South virtually in the position of a captive territory within the Union, that he had hoped the South would take up arms but feared it would not do so in time to be successful, and that with secession he strongly hoped the South would be permitted to go in peace to avoid the holocaust of civil war. We know that during the war period, believing that war issues might come before the Court and desiring to be ready for them, he busied himself with writing in private a series of opinions in which he found various war measures unconstitutional.[34]

In the Civil War period, therefore, the Supreme Court was again in a position where a redirection of trend was inevitable. President Lincoln prepared for the change by filling three Court vacancies with Northern men of undoubted loyalty to the Union. Congress helped by creating an additional judicial circuit in the Far West and a new Supreme Court position—one for a tenth justice—thereby permitting a fourth new appointment, that of Stephen J. Field. Chief Justice Taney died in 1864, to be replaced by Salmon P. Chase, the fifth and final Lincoln appointment. When in 1865 the death of another of the older members occurred, the vacancy was not filled, but the five Lincoln appointees now constituted a majority of the Court.

5 Although the appointment of new justices during and after the Civil War marked a break with the past, when a majority of the Court had leanings toward the proslavery side, it can hardly be said that any trend at all characterized the fifteen or twenty years immediately thereafter. Neither Chief Justice Chase nor his successor, Morrison R. Waite, attained effective leadership. For a time the Court, like the presidency, operated in the shadow of a Congress that was reaching out for power for its own organization. Congress defeated the President in the management of reconstruction and came close to ousting President Johnson on an impeachment charge. In enacting its reconstruction program it remembered the Court's unpopular action in striking down an act of Congress in the Dred Scott case, and it was in no mood to endure judicial opposition in reconstruction matters even though judicial personnel had been vastly changed. The Court sensed its own unpopularity resulting from the Dred Scott decision and sensed the determination of Congress not to accept judicial restraint. In case after case wherein a test of the constitutionality of reconstruction through operation of military governments in the South was sought, the Court managed to decide the cases at hand or to hold that it had no power in given situations, so as to avoid passing on the constitutional question.[35] In a habeas corpus case from a Southern circuit in which the Court heard arguments on the constitutionality of the reconstruction program, Congress initiated legislation to withdraw the appellate jurisdiction in the kind of case involved. The act was passed, vetoed by President Johnson, and passed over the veto. Although the case had been decided in conference the Court waited for the completion of congressional action and then announced that it had no jurisdiction.[36] In such cases it not only did not invite the opportunity to inject judicial determinations into political controversies but rather sought to avoid such injection.

If the Milligan decision showed the Court in retrospect ready to place a check on the expansion of military power in time of war,[37] while *Texas v. White* gave judicial ratification to the military determination that a state could not leave the Union,[38] the several cases dealing with the constitutionality of the legal tender acts of the war period showed the Court bogged down in the relation of the Constitution to monetary theory and to debtor-creditor controversies. The Court further damaged its own prestige when, having by a bare majority held that Congress could not make fiat money legal tender in payment of debts,[39] it followed the appointment of two new justices with a reversal of the earlier decision, again by a bare majority.[40] The reversal emphasized the fact that it was a matter of the opinions of individual persons, and not the guidance of an underlying body of fundamental law, that determined what could be done in an important economic field. In other words, it showed the Court operating not as a passive interpreter of clearly established law but as a largely political body. This demonstration was particularly unfortunate, coming as it did before the former prestige of the Court as an unbiased judicial body had been re-established.

The Lincoln appointees to the Court were wholeheartedly loyal to the Union and were friendly to the Negro. It might have been expected, therefore, that they would give full support to the enforcement of the Thirteenth, Fourteenth, and Fifteenth Amendments which were enacted to constitutionalize the victory achieved in the war. The Court as an institution had no commitment in behalf of the Negro, however, and although the members wished to see Negroes protected in their newly acquired rights, some of them were disturbed by the fanaticism of the Radical Congress as that Congress by continued use of military power, constitutional amendments, statutes, and impeachment proceedings sought to enforce its will not only to establish and maintain order but also to enhance its own power at the expense of the executive and judicial branches. Two remarks by Justice Samuel F. Miller in private correspondence illustrate the point:

> I think the progress of Congress in invading the functions of the executive and judicial branches of the government was only

> less dangerous than a return to power of the democratic party, with absolute control of the rebel states, governed by exasperated rebels, and their party in the north under their control, as they always have been, even during the rebellion.

And again,

> In the threatened collision between the legislative branch of the government and the executive and judicial branches I see consequences from which the cause of free government may never recover in my day.[41]

In the light of such concern it is not surprising that some of the justices turned toward a restricted interpretation of the postwar amendments, and congressional enactments based on them, and sought pretty much to restore the old federal balance between the nation and the states, in spite of the fact that the amendments stood as new constitutional limitations on the jurisdiction of the states. Arbitrary exercise of state power seemed to them no more dangerous than tyranny by federal legislators. This attitude, to be discussed more fully in Chapter V, caused narrow interpretation of amendments and statutes, and left Negroes deprived of much of the protection originally thought to have been afforded them.[42]

The same concern about the dangers of federal dominance over the states was reflected in early cases in which the Fourteenth Amendment was used to protect the rights of white people rather than Negroes. In the Slaughter-House Cases [43] the Court emasculated the provision that "No state shall make or enforce any law which shall abridge the privileges or immunities of citizens of the United States," by holding that the protection extended only to those rights Americans held peculiarly as citizens of the nation as distinguished from those they held as citizens of the states. It seems clear that the framers of the amendment had been concerned with giving protections that were broad and real, and not merely theoretical and narrow, but by nice textual examination the Court in a five-to-four decision denied protection against infringement by the states of rights generally regarded as belonging to all residents, or at least to all residents who were not aliens.

Yet although this interpretation of the privileges and immunities clause has in large part remained the law of the land until the present day, it was in the dissenting opinions that the trend of the near future was the more accurately forecast. Those opinions stressed the postwar amendments, and particularly the Fourteenth Amendment, as protecting civil rights generally, without reference to state-federal distinctions, with due process of law as an important source of that protection. The Slaughter-House Cases were concerned with a monopoly grant of the slaughtering business in a vast area in and around New Orleans, by which many butchers were denied the right to earn a livelihood. Justice Stephen J. Field thought that the Fourteenth Amendment protected the right. A number of quotations are relevant:

> It is nothing less than the question whether the recent Amendments to the Federal Constitution protect the citizens of the United States against the deprivation of their common rights by state legislation.[44]

> The provisions of the Fourteenth Amendment, which is properly a supplement to the Thirteenth, cover, in my judgment, the case before us, and inhibit any legislation which confers special and exclusive privileges like these under consideration. The Amendment was adopted to obviate objections which had been raised and pressed with great force to the validity of the civil rights act, and to place the common rights of the American citizens under the protection of the National government.[45]

> A citizen of a state is now only a citizen of the United States residing in that state. The fundamental rights, privileges, and immunities which belong to him as a free man and a free citizen, now belong to him as a citizen of the United States, and are not dependent on his citizenship of any state.[46]

> The privileges and immunities designated are those which of right belong to the citizens of all free governments.[47]

> [The Fourteenth Amendment] was intended to give practical effect to the declaration of 1776 of inalienable rights, rights which are the gift of the Creator; which the law does not confer, but only recognizes.[48]

Justice Joseph P. Bradley agreed with the Field position on the privileges and immunities of citizens and then brought the content of these privileges and immunities within the protection of the due process clause of the Fourteenth Amendment.

> In my view, a law which prohibits a large class of citizens from adopting a lawful employment, or from following a lawful employment previously adopted, does deprive them of liberty as well as property, without due process of law. Their right of choice is a portion of their liberty; their occupation is their property. Such a law also deprives those citizens of the equal protection of the laws, contrary to the last section.[49]

Justice Noah H. Swayne likewise thought that the statute violated privileges and immunities, due process, and equal protection clauses, noting that "By the Constitution, as it stood before the war, ample protection was given against oppression by the Union, but little was given against wrong and oppression by the states. That want was intended to be supplied by this Amendment." [50]

Herein was the promise of later incorporation of the great body of business rights of the American people into the area protected particularly by the due process clause of the Fourteenth Amendment. True, the protection came but slowly. In 1877 in *Munn v. Illinois*, seven members of the Court held that a state might regulate the rates of grain elevators even though the power of regulation was subject to abuse. "For protection against abuses by legislatures," said Chief Justice Waite, "the people must resort to the polls, and not to the courts." [51] In dissenting Justice Field had the support of only one colleague in his contention that the regulation violated the due process clause and in his denial of "the power of any legislature under our government to fix the price which any one shall receive for his property of any kind." [52] Yet by 1886 Chief Justice Waite was saying for the Court:

> From what has thus been said it is not to be inferred that this power of limitation or regulation is itself without limit. This power to regulate is not a power to destroy, and limitation is not the equivalent of confiscation. Under pretense of regulating

> fares and freights, the state cannot require a railroad corporation to carry persons or property without reward; neither can it do that which in law amounts to a taking of private property for public use without just compensation, or without due process of law.[53]

From this time onward for half a century Supreme Court decisions built out the range of due process protections to patrol the line at which state regulation impinged upon rights of property. From the 1880's until the 1930's, indeed, this type of activity constituted one of the major preoccupations of the Court.

6 It was during the half century following the late 1880's, and primarily in connection with Court action to curb government regulation of property, that New Deal spokesmen saw the departure of the Supreme Court from constitutional norms. Yet if in their sight there was such a departure, it did not take place along an even course. Although there was at no time any such influx of new personnel into positions of power as took place with the election of Andrew Jackson, and no major regional conflict such as that which culminated in the Civil War had to be resolved, the development of the United States into an industrial nation and into one of the leading world powers moved with the turbulence of a mighty stream, and the surges of public sentiment with respect to the character and scope of governmental activity were reflected in diverse expressions of doctrine by members of the Court. Trends in decisions moved now toward, now away from, the expansion of governmental regulatory and promotive power that marked the dominant public and governmental preference in the 1930's.

Due process, it can be said briefly at this point, marked one, though only one, of the important areas of judicial advance and retreat. Under due process protection, the extremes of liberty of contract got read into the Constitution, leading to the famous dissenting protest of Justice Holmes that "the 14th Amendment does not enact Mr. Herbert Spencer's Social Statics."[54] We are usually so intrigued by Justice Holmes' pungent phraseology and by his assumption of the relevance of the fact that the case was, as he said, "decided upon an economic theory which a large part of the country does not entertain,"[55] that we tend to forget the views of the majority of the Court and of many of the people. To them it was not a question whether the majority of the people adhered to the economic theory of the decision. It was not the responsibility of the Court to be democratic but to be constitutionally right, and to them constitutional rightness was on the side of sweeping liberty of contract, whatever the discomforts of those who were deprived of governmental paternalism.

Yet it was also in this period that the Court, impressed by the first of the now famous "Brandeis briefs," looked at the facts of the impact of hard work by women on the public welfare and held that with regard to women due process did not prevent government regulation of hours of labor,[56] even though liberty of contract was obviously restrained thereby. Having taken this step, the Court was able thereafter to uphold the regulation of hours for men as well as women,[57] but it balked at the fixing of minimum wages even for women,[58] deeming the field of prices one of peculiar sanctity that was not to be invaded by government under any ordinary circumstance. As for the field of "businesses affected with a public interest," in which, in line with *Munn v. Illinois,* prices might be regulated, the Court struggled mightily in its efforts to determine the limits of the category, finally abandoning it as a special category in 1934 and holding by a vote of five to four that there was nothing peculiarly sacred about prices if the public welfare required their regulation.[59] The course of doctrinal development, to repeat, was anything but straight and even, and by no means always was the trend inconsistent with the desires of those who believed in strong government.

The Supreme Court followed a similarly winding path in regard to the constitutionality of federal taxation. In 1881 the Court had held unanimously that a federal income tax could be collected as an indirect tax, that to be constitutionally levied it did not have to be apportioned among the several states according to population—an arrangement required for direct taxes which would have largely defeated the purpose of levying income taxes. But the property interests of the country, and some members of the Supreme Court, became frightened by the Populist movement of the early 1890's, or rather by the threat of socialism it was thought to offer. Moneyed interests set out to defeat in the Supreme Court a federal income tax measure that was passed by a Democratic Congress in 1894. The Court came to the rescue. Hearing arguments twice because the absence of one justice at the first argument left the Court evenly divided on some issues, it held in 1895 in *Pollock v. Farmers' Loan and Trust Company* [60] that the income tax could not be constitutionally levied as an indirect tax, thereby killing the measure. The motivation is found in the concurring statement of Justice Field:

> The present assault upon capital is but the beginning. It will be but the stepping-stone to others, larger and more sweeping, till our political contests will become a war of the poor against the rich; a war constantly growing in intensity and bitterness.[61]

He thought the evil ought to be scotched at the very beginning.

The close division of the Court, the shifting of position by one of the justices between the two arguments, and the general unpopularity of the decision brought discredit on the Court similar to that brought by the Dred Scott case and the Legal Tender Cases. Early changes in Court personnel led to the belief that the decision might be different if another case came before the Court, a belief that was encouraged by a decision upholding the collection of a graduated inheritance tax as an indirect tax.[62] Debate continued for a number of years over whether Congress should enact a new income tax measure to be presented to the Court or whether it should avoid embarrassment and further discredit to the Court by amending the Constitution. The amendment was decided upon, but before completion of its ratification in 1913 Congress levied a tax on corporations that was measured by income but was called an excise tax on the privilege of doing business, and the Court found the acts constitutional.[63] Thus new tax trends were determined by a combination of constitutional amendment and judicial adjustment.

The late 1890's brought further judicial travail with the Spanish-American War and the acquisition of additional noncontiguous territory for exploitation, temporary tutelage, or incorporation into the Union. The acquisition raised the question whether the Constitution followed the flag, whether the rights conferred by the Constitution extended to the inhabitants of the territory acquired. In what were informally known as the Insular Cases the Supreme Court divided in multiple directions but found a way to ratify the action taken, leading the great humorist of the time, Mr. Dooley, to confess continuing bewilderment as to whether the Constitution followed the flag but to assert sureness of one thing, that "th' Supreme Court follows th' illiction returns." [64]

The scope of federal power in relation to other countries was never in danger from Supreme Court decisions,[65] but the Court showed no such self-restraint where the internal issues of federalism and questions of the scope of property rights were involved. Here, as for example in the application of the federal commerce power, the varying predilections of the justices for limiting governmental power, for preserving a kind of balance between the states and the federal government, and for keeping property free from governmental restriction revealed themselves. To mention a few highlight situations: The Court struck down the Erdman Act of 1898, which had been calculated to prevent labor tie-ups similar to that in the Pullman Strike by ensuring the conditions necessary for bargaining between employers and labor unions for the settlement of disputes. Looking narrowly at the provision outlawing "yellow-dog contracts" rather than at its place in the program as a whole, the Court held that such contracts were within the rights protected by due process and that they did not in themselves constitute interstate commerce with which Congress could interfere.[66] Yet by 1930, in a case where the "yellow-dog" issue was not directly involved, the Court proved ready to look at the collective bargaining relationship as a whole, upholding provisions of the Railway Labor Act of 1926 that protected unionization of labor for collective bargaining purposes.[67] Here again the passing years disclosed a judicial drift in the direction of positions later emphasized by the New Deal.

The Court in 1913 gave support to the growing body of what is informally called federal police power legislation when it upheld the Mann Act prohibition of transportation of women in interstate commerce for immoral purposes. Surely, said Justice McKenna for the Court,

> if the facility of interstate transportation can be taken away from the demoralization of lotteries, the debasement of obscene literature, the contagion of diseased cattle or persons, the impurity of food and drugs, the like facility can be taken away from the systematic enticement to and the enslavement in prostitution and debauchery of women, and, more insistently, of girls.[68]

Yet the evils of child labor were regarded as quite a different matter. In 1918, by a vote of five to four, the Court held unconstitutional a federal statute prohibiting the shipment in interstate commerce of goods manufactured in any degree by the labor of children. The conditions of manufacture, the Court held, were within the police power of the states and not that of the federal government.[69] The scope of the power of Congress both to reach back to processes antedating actual shipment in interstate commerce and to reach forward to processes after shipment had taken place led to hot disputes during the New Deal period itself[70] and to ultimate broad interpretation thereafter.[71]

That offshoot of the commerce power, the Sherman Anti-Trust Act, of which it was said by Chief Justice Hughes, "As a charter of freedom the act has a generality and adaptability comparable to that found to be desirable in constitutional provisions,"[72] was a source of other cases reflecting divergent opinions concerning the scope of governmental powers and the relations of federalism. The laissez-faire Court of 1895 denied the reach of the statute, and incidentally of the commerce clause, back to combinations for the purpose of manufacture,[73] and seemed to threaten the devitalization of the statute. But later personnel yielded sufficiently to allow enforcement of the measure in broad areas.[74] Enforcement of the Sherman Act and its several amendments, with respect to combinations both of capital and of labor, was an area of great diversity of opinion for the Court until the program of the New Deal in some degree modified the direction of antitrust strategy.

In spite of its concern about protecting property rights against governmental invasion, the Supreme Court of the 1920's refused to interfere with procedures of the legislative and executive branches for the performance of their functions. In broad language it upheld the power of Congress to investigate whenever there was an assumed relation to the legislative process.[75] It gave broad interpretation to the President's pardoning power,[76] and, more important, to his power to remove from office employees of the executive branch of the government. In *Myers v. United States,*[77] decided in 1926, with former President, now Chief Justice, Taft speaking for the Court in a six-to-three decision, the Court upheld the power of the President to remove a postmaster who had been appointed for a specified term. Taft wrote the opinion of the Court, however, in such a way as to extend the removal power not only to purely executive and administrative officers but officers with quasi-legislative and quasi-judicial functions as well. The decision paved the way for one of the major clashes between the Court and the administration in the New Deal period, when after the retirement of Chief Justice Taft the Court backtracked with respect to officers not strictly executive and administrative and denied the President the power to remove a member of the Federal Trade Commission,[78] thereby excluding the personnel of a vast assortment of federal agencies from presidential control.

7 The story of the New Deal conflict that led to the constitutional renaissance discussed by Attorney General Jackson is too well known to require more than mention here. The Court, which from 1790 through 1934 had struck down only some sixty-six statutes or parts of statutes, placed its negative on eleven measures in the years 1935-36 alone, curbed the President's removal power, and demonstrated a continuing pattern of old beliefs by denying a state the power to fix minimum wages.[79] To an unprecedented degree the Supreme Court frustrated attempts at strong and effective crisis government both by the legislative and executive branches in Washington and by the states. This conflict between the Court and other agencies of government led to the similarly unprecedented attempt to pack the Court with enough new members to ensure the possibility of support for government programs.

It is likewise a familiar story that even as the President was waging his campaign for court reform, with Attorney General Jackson playing a prominent part, a number of cases were decided in which important federal measures were upheld, creating the impression that New Deal enactments would be upheld if and when Congress enacted some that were constitutional; a reversal of the minimum-wage decision seemed to promise increased leeway for the states as well. Furthermore, the retirement of Justice Van Devanter marked the beginnings of changes in personnel without the necessity of increasing the number of justices. From this time on, strategic past decisions that stood in the way of exercise of broad governmental powers were overruled one by one or devitalized by interpretation, giving us what Justice Jackson called a renaissance in constitutional law.

Yet if the events of the late 1930's constituted a renaissance in constitutional interpretation, or a revolution, or a tidal wave of change in contrast with earlier waves of lesser dimensions, what has thus far been said demonstrates the fact that the transitions were of degree only. Constitutional law in the United States has always been in transition. To return to the point made by Justice Cardozo about the judicial process: thus far there has been no period in American history when the judicial function could be imitative or static. Something more has always been required than merely "diligence and memory and normal powers of reasoning." [80] The judicial function has had to be "dynamic and creative." Although for novel situations competitive analogies have provided hints and clues, precedents have been lacking with "authoritative commands," and justices have tended to differ among themselves in terms of all sorts of factors. So it is that we have had professional strife on the Court over critical steps in the development of law, with judicial positions varying in terms of streams of ideas, backgrounds of tradition, sentiments dominant at the time of making particular appointments, the interactions of particular justices one upon the other, and no doubt many additional considerations.

For those who find disillusioning the lack of stability in our constitutional development, it is worth remembering that within our constitutional period our population has grown from some 3,000,000 to 164,000,000. The frontier of settlement has moved from the Appalachians to the Pacific Coast and islands far beyond. Emphasis has shifted from small agriculture to big industry. And whereas we began as a power almost too insignificant to attract major attention save as we might be a factor in the disputes between other powers, we are now one of the great powers of the world. Such sweeping transitions put torturing strains on the development of a constitutional system.

Furthermore, unaccustomed to thinking in terms of the tremendous time spans of Europe and Asia, we tend to ignore the brevity of our constitutional experience and to expect more of the stability produced by time than it is possible to expect in a country of such brief experience. Some enumerations help to point up the vastness of changes within brief periods. Speaking loosely in the round figures of decades, it is now only twenty years since the Roosevelt attempt to pack the Court; forty years since the holding that the commerce power did not enable Congress to prohibit child labor; fifty years since the holding that a state could not restrict hours of labor in bakeshops; sixty years since Congress was denied the power to collect unapportioned income taxes; one hundred years since the holding that Congress could not exclude slavery from the territories and the assertion that Negroes could not have constitutional rights as citizens; one hundred fifty years since the Court first invalidated an act of Congress; one hundred eighty years since the drafting of the Constitution; one hundred ninety years since the Declaration of Independence; and two hundred years since the Albany Congress of 1754, where the first formal discussion of possible unity of action by the American colonies of the British king took place, at a time when there was no real thought of the assertion of American sovereignty.

Two hundred years ago, in other words, there was not only no Supreme Court and no body of American constitutional law: there was no Constitution and no Union. There was territory that in the sense of sovereignty belonged partly to Britain and partly to other European powers. There were people who owed allegiance to the British king and other sovereigns. There was especially the English common law with its deeply engrained patterns, and there were structures of government primarily of the kind with which English people were familiar. The American colonists took the territory and the people and the law and traditions and wove them into a nation. The nation adopted a Constitution in largely undefined language, which the Supreme Court was to interpret in the light of the traditions and basic assumptions of the people.

Such has been the task of the Court throughout its history. It has sought always, or almost always, to find and declare stability and certainty in the law. But at an overwhelming rate of speed conditions have changed, desires have changed, and our conceptions of the good society to be governed under the Constitution have been transformed. As to the true path of the law, the Court quite as much as the people has often been in a state of bewilderment. Yet cases have had to be decided whether judges were bewildered or not, and the decision of cases has given us new extensions of law, sometimes in spite of ourselves and in spite of the judges who decided them.

Constitutional evolution, furthermore, it must be said, though said tritely, did not stop with the constitutional "renaissance" after the New Deal struggle. Life goes on with war and cold war and economic stress and strain, and new litigation necessitates new decisions. The ensuing chapters will deal with the efforts of the renovated Supreme Court to find the path of justice and declare it in terms of the Constitution and of those broad federal statutes that themselves have, in the language of Chief Justice Hughes about the Sherman Act, already quoted, "a generality and adaptability comparable to that found to be desirable in constitutional provisions." [81] We turn now to the current or relatively current period, with emphasis on prevailing judicial attitudes toward restraints on government, and particularly those restraints that come within the province of "due process of law."

II *Checkreins upon Government*

Before beginning discussion of the central theme of this chapter, it seems well to note a commonplace fact that we too often forget. It is only in connection with the settlement of disputes, with the decision of cases, that it is, in the language of Chief Justice Marshall, "emphatically the province and duty of the judicial department to say what the law is." [1] The legislative and executive branches of the government as well as the judiciary are established by the Constitution and are subject to the restraints of the Constitution. Their officers and employees take an oath to uphold the Constitution. Congress must interpret the Constitution, must estimate the scope of its constitutional powers when it sets out to enact legislation, and must take into account the relevant constitutional prohibitions. The President and his subordinate officers and employees likewise look on the Constitution as well as on the statutes as the central source of power and of restrictions on the exercise of power. The oath taken by legislative and executive officers to support the Constitution is just as relevant to constitutional enforcement as that taken by the judiciary, of which Chief Justice Marshall made so much in *Marbury v. Madison.*[2] The states also have their rightful place in our constitutional system, with powers and prerogatives on the one hand and on the other hand obligations to observe the "keep-off" signs of the Constitution.

It is true, of course, that there is an important difference between the states and the legislative and executive branches of the federal government in that the former derive their powers from their own constitutions or from their own sources in their people, whereas the latter derive their powers, and indeed their very existence, from the federal Constitution. The point here involved, however, is that notwithstanding the differences, all of them have an obligation to obey the Constitution in its relevant provisions and to estimate as accurately as possible what those provisions mean. They cannot be constantly running to the federal judiciary with the host of questions of interpretation that inevitably arise. They can get judicial answers only through cases or controversies, which constitute an area not of first but of last resort.

Furthermore, what has here been said needs to be restated in part in support of another commonplace fact that is likewise often disregarded. In spite of the importance of the Constitution as an instrument for preventing evils, it was not drafted and does not exist primarily for the purpose of defining and enforcing prohibitions. It was drafted to establish a government and prescribe the mode of its operation. It was and is a positive document, not a negative document. Any complete and comprehensive study of it must put its emphasis on the Constitution as a source of power and not as a barrier to the exercise of power. This necessity becomes all the greater as the positive state comes into realization, as more and more of the processes of society come to flow from, or to be regulated by, government. In a multiple-purpose constitutional system like ours even the judiciary, notwithstanding its responsibility for enforcing the flat negatives of our supreme law, is primarily preoccupied not with the negatives as such but with determining, amid what Justice Holmes called "the quiet of a storm centre," [3] the outer boundaries of the exercise of powers that are basically legitimate. The judiciary refines and when necessary corrects constitutional interpretation, in the context of the interactions of the three branches and of the federal system, almost always in situations where some agency of federal or state government has engaged in action that stems ultimately from some legitimate area of governmental power.

In setting barriers against the exercise of illegitimate powers, however, and against the improper exercise of powers that are legitimate, the Constitution does include important prohibitions, both against the federal government and against the states. Although the states and the federal legislative and executive branches must operate with an eye directed toward these prohibitions, it is the judiciary that determines finally whether they have been observed. Our purpose here is to deal briefly with the prohibitions en masse and then to follow only a few of the many threads of judicial interpretations.

1 Most of the specific prohibitions laid upon government by the Constitution are pretty well grouped. In the original Constitution most of the prohibitions against federal action were listed in Section 9 of Article I. Denied here was the power to stop the slave trade before 1808, to suspend the privilege of the writ of habeas corpus except under restricted circumstances, to enact bills of attainder or ex post facto laws, to collect direct taxes without apportionment according to population, to discriminate among the ports of the several states, to spend federal money except under specified restrictions, to grant titles of nobility, or to receive foreign gifts ex-

cept with the consent of Congress. Although some of these prohibitions are important, and have been the basis of important judicial decisions, they have not resulted in heavy litigation. It was not until 1867 that one of them, the bill of attainder and ex post facto clause, brought a Supreme Court decision of unconstitutionality.[4] That clause and those having to do with the writ of habeas corpus and with direct taxes have been responsible for most of the work the section brought to the federal courts.

Section 10 of Article I included many provisions restricting or denying power to the states with respect to foreign relations and foreign trade and contract and monetary matters, here again with prohibitions against bills of attainder and ex post facto laws. Prohibitions against impairing the obligation of contracts and issuing bills of credit gave rise to important Supreme Court decisions in the Marshall period,[5] and here again the attainder and ex post facto provisions became important at the close of the Civil War.

But most of the more drastic, and at any rate the more controversial, restrictions upon government, both federal and state, came in later years with the adoption of constitutional amendments. The first eight amendments, commonly known as the Bill of Rights and including much of the content of the bills of rights in the state constitutions, placed restraints only on the federal government. The First Amendment referred specifically to Congress and the Seventh to the courts of the United States, and the Supreme Court held many years after their adoption that the other amendments, which failed to specify the governments referred to, restrained only the exercise of federal power.[6] These amendments ranged all the way from the guarantee of freedom of religion, speech, press, and assembly in the First Amendment to protection against cruel and unusual punishments in the Eighth, with the due process clause of the Fifth Amendment destined to loom large in future litigation.

The post-Civil War amendments, the Thirteenth, Fourteenth, and Fifteenth, were written in part to restrain the federal government as well as the states, but the impact was primarily on the latter, with the due process clause and its lesser sibling, the equal protection clause of the Fourteenth Amendment, looming large. The Nineteenth Amendment extended to voting discrimination on the basis of sex the ban that the Fifteenth had placed on race discrimination in this field, a ban applying to both state and federal governments.

Practically all these prohibitions, whether laid on the federal government or the states or on both, and whether included in the original Constitution or in amendments thereto, have one thing in common. They are deemed to have now, or at any rate to have had at some time, some rootage in natural law or natural right. Many of them have their source in the English common law, where a kind of sanctity derives from a combination of custom, "right reason," and the doctrines of Christianity. The purpose is the doing of justice, of justice that can be achieved only if some things are done by the appropriate procedures and only if some activities on the part of government are forbidden altogether.

2 Supreme Court attitudes toward these prohibitions can be most effectively summarized by fixing attention on the requirement of due process of law, and on the controversy over the extent to which due process encompasses other prohibitions written in more specific language. That is, we shall deal with the question whether due process encompasses all the prohibitions of the first eight amendments, or merely some of them, and whether it makes those encompassed applicable to the states. It is an old story that due process terminology dates back at least to the fourteenth century and encompasses the subject matter of the "law of the land" of the Magna Carta of the year 1215. For Americans it had the sanctity of age and of fundamental rightness. The Supreme Court in 1856 asserted:

> The article is a restraint on the legislative as well as on the executive and judicial powers of the government, and cannot

be so construed as to leave Congress free to make any process "due process of law," by its mere will.[7]

As for the determination of due process under the Constitution, it must not be in conflict with the provisions of the Constitution.

If found not to be so, we must look to those settled usages and modes of proceeding existing in the common and statute law of England, before the emigration of our ancestors, and which are shown not to have been unsuited to their civil and political condition by having been acted on by them after the settlement of this country.[8]

Before the adoption of the Fourteenth Amendment it was not assumed that the due process clause of the Fifth Amendment included any of the other provisions of the first eight amendments. If due process had such breadth of content, the inclusion of the other prohibitions in separate language would have been "superfluous and inappropriate," [9] and would have betrayed the Constitution as a less perfect document than it was then assumed to be. But after the Fourteenth Amendment made due process a federal restriction on the states, it was widely urged, as by counsel and by Justice Harlan dissenting in *Hurtado v. California* [10] in 1884, that at least some of the non-due process restrictions of the first eight amendments were made applicable to the states by the due process clause of the Fourteenth Amendment. But the Supreme Court here held that due process did not make indictment by grand jury a necessary preliminary to a criminal trial in a state, even though such a requirement had been entrenched in English custom and was imposed on the federal government in specific language in the Fifth Amendment. Said Justice Matthews for the Court:

any legal proceeding enforced by public authority, whether sanctioned by age and custom, or newly devised in the discretion of the legislative power, in furtherance of the general public good, which regards and preserves these principles of liberty and justice, must be held to be due process of law.[11]

The decision thereby trimmed from due process some of the detail of the first eight amendments—detail that was never included in its entirety by the majority of the Court—but left the requirement that procedures must be in furtherance of the public good and preserve "principles of liberty and justice." In effect, therefore, due process of law was to be measured by the natural law concepts of the members of the Supreme Court.

From the Hurtado decision in 1884 until *Palko v. Connecticut* [12] in 1937, the Supreme Court wrestled in case after case over the extent to which the due process clause of the Fourteenth Amendment made applicable to the states the content of the first eight amendments. As summarized by Justice Cardozo in the Palko case, the following items seemed not to be included if the fundamentals of protection were otherwise given: indictment by grand jury, double jeopardy, jury trial, protection against unreasonable search and seizures, or the right of defendants to be confronted by witnesses.

> On the other hand, the due process clause of the Fourteenth Amendment may make it unlawful for a state to abridge by its statutes the freedom of speech which the First Amendment safeguards against encroachment by the Congress . . . or the like freedom of the press . . . or the free exercise of religion . . . or the right of peaceable assembly, without which speech would be unduly trammeled . . . or the right of one accused of crime to the benefit of counsel. . . . In these and other situations immunities that are valid as against the federal government by force of the specific pledges of particular amendments have been found to be implicit in the concept of ordered liberty, and thus, through the Fourteenth Amendment, become valid as against the states.[13]

The distinction, Justice Cardozo thought, was a clear one. Restrictions of the first eight amendments that the Court did not include within due process might have value and importance, but they were "not of the very essence of a scheme of ordered liberty. To abolish them is not to violate a 'principle of justice so rooted in the traditions and conscience of our people as to be ranked as fundamental.'"[14] The key words now were "ordered liberty," "traditions," "conscience," and "fundamental." All these terms were of the essence of natural law interpretation. They were important instruments of constitutional law to the extent that there was general agreement as to their content both among the people and among the members of the Supreme Court. When either the people generally or the justices were sharply divided, or when there was keen distrust among the members of the Court, the concepts were blurred as instruments of measurement. The Court, without guidance from the Constitution itself, had erected a hierarchy of values for measuring constitutional provisions, labeling some of them as more fundamental, as of greater worth and therefore of wider constitutional extent, than other provisions. It was inevitable that members of the Court should not only disagree over the arrangement of the hierarchy of values but should at times challenge the validity of the hierarchical device itself.

Before turning to the story of that challenge, however, further discussion of due process as a restriction on government regulation of property, as begun in the preceding chapter, will be helpful. Justice Stephen J. Field, one of the principal architects of this wing of due process protection, quoted in part the eloquent statement of John Adams:

> Property is surely a right of mankind as really as liberty. . . . The moment the idea is admitted into society, that property is not as sacred as the laws of God, and that there is not a force of law and public justice to protect it, anarchy and tyranny commence.[15]

The Supreme Court of the 1880's and 1890's worked this concept into the law of the land, with the result that, in the language of Edward S. Corwin, "The country was presented with a new, up-to-date version of natural law." [16] The concept was applied not only in the specialized field of rate regulation but in relation to property generally, where "liberty of contract" became the specialized slogan of due process for inhibiting state action.[17] By means of due process in its various applications, the Supreme Court served during the late nineteenth century and the first third of this century as the special defender of property rights, at a time when state legislatures and Congress were placing more and more restrictions on the use of property in the interest of the public welfare. This topic provided much of the subject matter for the "splinter movement," labeled in the comments of the late 1920's as "Holmes, Brandeis and Stone dissenting." The growing public sentiment in behalf of more extensive control of property made itself felt among other justices as well, however, leading to the demolition of the public interest concept as a restricted and exceptional area wherein price could be regulated.[18] Incidentally demolished also was the so-called rule of *Smyth v. Ames*,[19] that rate regulation must not deny the opportunity to earn a fair return on the fair value of the property involved—with a highly indefinite sliding-scale method of determining value. Said Justice Stone for the Court in 1942, "the Constitution does not bind rate-making bodies to the service of any particular formula or combination of formulas." [20] Two years later Justice Douglas for the Court dispensed with the fair-value concept by holding that the fact that a regulation reduced the value of property did not invalidate the regulation, and that "the heart of the matter is that rates cannot be made to depend upon 'fair value' when the value of the going enterprise depends on earnings under whatever rates may be anticipated." [21]

3 Yet as these and other cases were being decided to curb the use of due process to prevent governmental interference with property rights, sentiment was building for use of the concept to protect personal and civil rights. The Holmes, Brandeis, and Stone contingent here took the lead. In the matter of restrictions on property rights Justice Holmes could say:

> There is nothing that I more deprecate than the use of the 14th Amendment beyond the absolute compulsion of its words to

> prevent the making of social experiments that an important part of the community desires, in the insulated chambers afforded by the several states, even though the experiments may seem futile or even noxious to me and to those whose judgment I most respect.[22]

Yet he made no such ringing statements when civil liberties were threatened by the states.[23] Justice Brandeis was a defender of state powers where property was involved, but he was willing to employ due process to protect civil liberties, saying, for example:

> Prohibitory legislation has repeatedly been held invalid, because unnecessary, where the denial of liberty involved was that of engaging in a particular business. The power of the courts to strike down an offending law are no less when the interests involved are not property rights, but the fundamental personal rights of free speech and assembly.[24]

In upholding a state regulation of insurance a majority of the Court had said incidentally in 1922, under circumstances such that Justices Holmes and Brandeis could not dissent without breaking up the majority, that "neither the 14th Amendment nor any other provision of the Constitution of the United States imposes upon the states any restrictions about 'freedom of speech' or the 'liberty of silence.' "[25] In the Gitlow case of 1925, however, the Court noted:

> For present purposes we may and do assume that freedom of speech and of the press—which are protected by the 1st Amendment from abridgement by the Congress—are among the fundamental personal rights and "liberties" protected by the due process clause of the 14th Amendment from impairment by the states.[26]

By 1925, in other words, the majority of the Court was willing to admit that due process protected civil liberties as well as property rights against state action. The next step was a further shift in position to an assumption, already held apparently by Justices Holmes and Brandeis, that civil liberties had in due process a protection even greater than that given to property rights.

The fact that civil liberties eventually attained a "preferred position" by contrast with property rights is to be gathered as much from "circumstantial evidence" as from direct statements of a majority of the Court. A number of intervening cases led up to the Palko case discussed above. In that case, although the distinction was between fundamental rights protected by due process and others deemed less fundamental that were not, Justice Cardozo took occasion, along with presenting the First Amendment as included in due process, to discuss the prime importance of freedom of speech and thought.

> Of that freedom one may say that it is the matrix, the indispensable condition, of nearly every other form of freedom. With rare aberrations a pervasive recognition of that truth can be traced in our history, political and legal. So it has come about that the domain of liberty, withdrawn by the Fourteenth Amendment from encroachment by the states, has been enlarged by latter-day judgments to include liberty of the mind as well as liberty of action.[27]

Even though the contrast directly in mind was not that between personal liberty and property rights, the essence of the concept of primacy is to be found in the quotation.

The subject came more directly to the fore a few months later in the Carolene Products case when the Court upheld federal regulation of milk shipped in interstate commerce. In upholding the restriction on property rights, Justice Stone, speaking for the Court, included what has become a well-known footnote, one better known and more important than the text of the opinion. The footnote read as follows:

> There may be narrower scope for operation of the presumption of constitutionality when legislation appears on its face to be within a specific prohibition of the Constitution, such as those of the first ten amendments, which are deemed equally specific when held to be embraced within the Fourteenth. . . .
>
> It is unnecessary to consider now whether legislation which restricts those political processes which can ordinarily be expected to bring about repeal of undesirable legislation, is to be subjected to more exact judicial scrutiny under the general

scrutiny of the Fourteenth Amendment than are most other types of legislation. . . .

Nor need we inquire whether similar considerations enter into the review of states directed at particular religions . . . or national . . . or racial minorities . . . whether prejudice against discrete and insular minorities may be a special condition, which tends seriously to curtail the operation of those political processes ordinarily to be relied upon to protect minorities, and which may call for a correspondingly more searching judicial inquiry.[28]

Here was a suggestion of the primacy of personal rights under the Fourteenth Amendment based not so much on the position that those rights were, in the language of Justice Cardozo, the indispensable condition of nearly every other form of freedom, as on the ground that their more specific protection against the federal government in the first eight amendments gave them that specific protection against the states through the due process clause of the Fourteenth Amendment. In other words, the intrinsic primacy of personal rights and the question of the interrelations between the first eight amendments and the Fourteenth Amendment were now hopelessly entangled. For the purposes of this discussion it is not important that the footnote in question was written in large part by Justice Stone's law clerk and that it was "not unusual for Stone to allow his law clerks to use footnotes as trial balloons for meritorious ideas."[29] Stone adopted the footnote as his own, and it had repercussions far beyond the scope of many passages of text. The man who in connection with the regulation of property had reminded his brethren that "courts are concerned only with the power to enact statutes, not with their wisdom," and that as to courts "the only check upon our own exercise of power is our own sense of self-restraint,"[30] was now suggesting a mode of interpretation to justify increased judicial power with respect to personal liberty.

In the Barnette case of 1943, the second of the two flag-salute cases to come before the Court, Justice Jackson for the Court used words that could be interpreted as implying the primacy of personal liberty along with the measurement of due process of the Fourteenth Amendment by the content of the first eight amendments. Defending the right to dissent, he noted: "Those who begin coercive elimination of dissent soon find themselves exterminating dissenters. Compulsory unification of opinion achieves only the unanimity of the graveyard." [31] As for the content of due process, he asserted:

> In weighing arguments of the parties it is important to distinguish between the due process clause of the Fourteenth Amendment as an instrument for transmitting the principles of the First Amendment and those cases in which it is applied for its own sake. The test of legislation which collides with the Fourteenth Amendment, because it also collides with the principles of the First, is much more definite than the test when only the Fourteenth is involved. Much of the vagueness of the due process clause disappears when the specific prohibitions of the First become its standard.[32]

The decision brought from Justice Frankfurter a dissenting opinion paraphrasing Justice Stone's warning quoted above; he said: "The admonition that judicial self-restraint alone limits arbitrary exercise of our authority is relevant every time we are asked to nullify legislation." [33] Stone had voiced the warning in connection with property rights, however, whereas here personal rights were at stake. The reasoning employed by the Court seemed to make fully applicable to the states the prohibitions of the First Amendment, which specifically provided merely that "Congress shall make no law . . . ," and to make them as applicable as if the First Amendment had provided specifically that "No state shall. . . ." In 1945, indeed, referring to "the preferred place given in our scheme to the great, the indispensable democratic freedoms secured by the First Amendment," the Court struck down a state statute as violative of the First Amendment without mentioning the Fourteenth, further saying: "That priority gives these liberties a sanctity and a sanction not permitting dubious intrusions." [34]

The combined doctrine of the primacy of personal liberties and the applicability of the Bill of Rights to the states (whether directly or through the Fourteenth Amendment) was reasserted in case after case,[35] as a curb on the presumption of the constitutionality of legislation. From the point of view of its purpose, the doctrine of primacy was vulnerable in that it was possible to claim virtue by paying it lip service while at the same time finding grounds for upholding restrictive legislation.[36] It was highly unpopular with Justice Frankfurter, who said of the phrase "the preferred position of freedom of speech":

> I deem it a mischievous phrase, if it carries the thought, which it may subtly imply, that any law touching communication is infected with presumptive invalidity. . . . I say the phrase is mischievous because it radiates a constitutional doctrine without avowing it.[37]

Although he admitted that the doctrine had at times had the support of a majority of the Court, he criticized the doctrine of preferred position as having originated "with the casualness of a footnote," and as engendering the belief that "there is a constitutional principle, expressed by those attractive but imprecise words, prohibiting restriction upon utterance unless it creates a situation of 'imminent' peril against which legislation may guard." [38]

The doctrinal controversy here became entangled with interpretation of the "clear and present danger" doctrine, which will be discussed in Chapter III. Suffice it for the moment to say that for the majority of the Court the primacy of civil liberties faded into the background with the growing intensity of the cold war and with changes in personnel on the Court, but that it is by no means necessarily a dead issue at the present time. The Court, in other words, has been able to shift from what was in effect a position that property rights have primacy under the Constitution to a position that primacy lies in personal rights, without formal constitutional change but with enormous effect on the pattern of constitutional doctrine and on the practical matter of the impact of judicial review on challenged legislation.

4 In the meantime a closely related controversy was raging among Supreme Court justices. The question was this: if freedom of speech and related freedoms were constitutionally protected against the states, did the protection derive from the due process clause of the Fourteenth Amendment or from the fact that the Fourteenth Amendment, without specific reference to its due process clause, made the whole Bill of Rights directly applicable to the states? As noted above, the Supreme Court in one important case avoided that question by treating the First Amendment as a direct restriction upon the states without specific reference to the Fourteenth Amendment.[39] It was generally obvious, however, that the phrase "Congress shall make no law" could not be converted into "No state shall" without resort to some intermediary, and the obvious intermediary was some aspect of the Fourteenth Amendment. To Justice Frankfurter and a majority of the Court, furthermore, it was the due process clause of the amendment that provided the linkage. To Justice Black and a minority of other justices it was not the due process clause but the Fourteenth Amendment as a whole, or the whole first section, that made applicable to the states the basic restrictions which the Bill of Rights placed on the federal government.

The controversy was important because of its implications as to the power of the Supreme Court to expand or contract the scope of protection it might give against state action. If the Fourteenth Amendment made the Bill of Rights applicable to the states, and if the due process clause itself was restricted merely to matters of procedure, as Justice Black contended that it should be, then at least to the extent of the language of the first eight amendments, the power of the Court over state action was spelled out. On the other hand, if what a state might do was restricted merely by the due process clause, with the giving and withholding of content from that clause dictated by the mood of the times or the predilections of individual justices, then there was little certainty in this aspect of constitutional law, and there was great temptation for the exercise of arbitrary judicial power. Yet the deflation of due process and the reading of the Bill of Rights into the Fourteenth Amendment would require considerable rewriting of history and redirection of Supreme Court decisions.

The doctrinal controversy between Justices Frankfurter and Black came out into the open in *Adamson v. California*,[40] decided in 1947. In a sense it was a battle on the sidelines of that case, since neither wrote the opinion of the Court. Justice Frankfurter wrote a concurring opinion, which was in large part an attempt to answer a dissenting opinion by Justice Black. The reader almost loses sight of the opinion of the Court written by Justice Reed, competent performance though it is, in the pyrotechnic side show put on by the two warriors. Almost completely overlooked, too, is Admiral Dewey Adamson, a Negro awaiting execution of the death sentence upon losing his case in the Supreme Court—as he did lose it by a vote of five to four. Forgotten now is a family heritage that led to his being named "Admiral Dewey," after the hero of Manila, or after some person who half a century earlier had been named for the Admiral. Lost is the story of a life of crime, of prison sentences previously served, of a passion for the collection of women's stocking tops, presumably only of stockings that had been worn. Lost is the story of the body of a murdered woman stripped of stockings but with one remaining stocking, with the top missing, under the body, the story of the lamp cord drawn tightly around her neck, and the story also of missing jewelry and of a burglar's breaking through a garbage compartment into the kitchen of the woman's apartment in pursuit of jewelry she had unwisely displayed.

The case was conducted, indeed—and rightly, of course, in terms of the law—almost as if the murdered woman had never lived and without direct reference to the fact that the defendant was about to die. In speaking for the Court Justice Reed merely followed *Twining v. New Jersey,* decided in

1908, in which it had been held that the Constitution did not forbid a state to compel a defendant to be a witness against himself at his own trial.[41] Such was the question here. Adamson had not testified at his trial. But the law of California permitted the prosecutor and the judge to call to the attention of the jury the failure to testify, leaving the jury to draw its own inferences. In appealing the decision Adamson's counsel contended that he could not reasonably testify, since if he did so the prosecution would be permitted to draw out the fact of his previous convictions and thereby prejudice the jury against him. Yet in view of the right of the prosecutor and the judge to call attention to the failure to testify, it was contended that Adamson was in effect being made to testify against himself and that he was thus having his life taken without due process of law.

The Twining case provided a precedent immediately in point, as Justice Black admitted, and Justice Reed had no difficulty in showing that the degree of self-incrimination here compelled did not violate due process, in spite of the fact that in a federal court the decision would have been governed by the provision that no person should "be compelled in any criminal case to be a witness against himself." Justice Black was challenging the Twining decision itself and the procedure whereby, as portrayed by Justice Cardozo in the Palko case, discussed above,[42] some of the provisions of the Bill of Rights were held to apply to the states through the due process clause and others were held not to apply. He contended that the first section of the Fourteenth Amendment made all of them applicable, including the one here involved, which protected against enforced self-incrimination. He could not "consider the Bill of Rights to be an outworn 18th Century 'strait jacket' as the Twining opinion did."[43] Furthermore,

> I fear to see the consequences of the Court's practice of substituting its own concepts of decency and fundamental justice for the language of the Bill of Rights as its point of departure in interpreting and enforcing that Bill of Rights. If the choice must be between the selective process of the Palko decision

applying some of the Bill of Rights to the states, or the Twining rule applying none of them, I would choose the Palko selective process. But rather than accept either of these choices, I would follow what I believe was the original purpose of the Fourteenth Amendment—to extend to all the people of the nation the complete protection of the Bill of Rights.[44]

With a profound disrespect for natural law reasoning, which he nowhere defined but which he equated with the Court's weaving back and forth in its interpretation of due process of law, Black demanded the abandonment of this mode of arrival at Court decisions.

I further contend that the "natural law" formula which the Court uses to reach its conclusion in this case should be abandoned as an incongruous excrescence on our Constitution. I believe that formula to be itself a violation of our Constitution, in that it subtly conveys to courts, at the expense of legislatures, ultimate power over public policies in fields where no specific provision of the Constitution limits legislative power.[45]

Justice Frankfurter could not be expected to like the label of "incongruous excrescence" on a mode of reasoning that had his full approval. In answering the attack and in defending the Twining decision he committed himself to the position that some decisions of the Court had more validity as precedents than others—"Decisions of this Court do not have equal intrinsic authority"[46]—and, as he cited names of outstanding participants in the Twining and Palko decisions, to an aristocracy of elite justices among the many who had served on the Court. He found a vulnerable point in Justice Black's argument, saying:

Even the boldest innovator would shrink from suggesting to more than half the states that they may no longer initiate prosecutions without indictment by grand jury, or that thereafter all the states of the Union must furnish a jury of twelve for every case involving a claim above twenty dollars.[47]

If some but not all the restrictions of the first eight amendments were to be applied to the states, some standard of selection was needed. He thought natural law reasoning not inappropriate.

> In the history of thought "natural law" has a much longer and much better founded meaning and justification than such subjective selection of the first eight amendments for incorporation into the Fourteenth. If all that is meant is that due process contains within itself certain minimum standards which are "of the very essence of a scheme of ordered liberty," *Palko v. Connecticut*, . . . putting upon this Court the duty of applying these standards from time to time, then we have merely arrived at the insight which our predecessors long ago expressed.[48]

To him the Fourteenth Amendment did not comprehend the specific provisions of the first eight amendments and was not confined to them. Furthermore, the due process clause of the Fourteenth Amendment had a specific potency, just as did the parallel clause in the Fifth Amendment. The clause had the same meaning in both amendments. In independent phrases the Fifth Amendment required that indictments be made by grand jury and forbade double jeopardy and compulsory self-incrimination. Could the authors be accused of writing into the amendment a meaningless clause? Here again was the contention that the Constitution could not be assumed to contain surplus verbiage. Yet, oddly enough in view of this argument, Justice Frankfurter was among those who believed that the due process clause of the Fourteenth Amendment incorporated the same subject matter as was included in the First Amendment.

However that may be, the question as Justice Frankfurter saw it was not whether the California court had violated the self-incrimination clause of the Fifth Amendment but whether it had denied due process as forbidden by the Fourteenth.

> Judicial review of that guaranty of the Fourteenth Amendment inescapably imposes upon this Court an exercise of judgment upon the whole course of the proceedings in order to ascertain whether they offend those canons of decency and fairness which express the notions of justice of English-speaking peoples even toward those charged with the most heinous offenses. These standards of justice are not authoritatively formulated anywhere as though they were prescriptions in a pharmacopoeia. But neither does the application of the due process clause imply that judges are wholly at large. The judicial judgment in ap-

plying the due process clause must move within the limits of accepted notions of justice and is not to be based upon the idiosyncrasies of a merely personal judgment.[49]

The clash between Justices Black and Frankfurter over the proper mode of determining the scope of personal rights protected by the Constitution provoked widespread discussion. The most thorough analysis was that published by Charles Fairman and Stanley Morrison in the *Stanford Law Review* for December, 1949, under the over-all title, "Does the Fourteenth Amendment Incorporate the Bill of Rights?" The authors pretty well demonstrated that Justice Black's search for the original intent of the framers, like that of other students, was at best inconclusive. It became clear, in short, that the justice was attempting to make history prove the thesis he was advancing.

In the Adamson case Black had the full concurrence of Justice Douglas. Justice Murphy, with the concurrence of Justice Rutledge, took from Black's position all the protection he could get for personal rights, but he himself went further, calling on the content of due process as well.

> I agree that the specific guarantees of the Bill of Rights should be carried over intact into the first section of the Fourteenth Amendment. But I am not prepared to say that the latter is entirely and necessarily limited by the Bill of Rights.[50]

With the deaths of Justices Murphy and Rutledge the advocates of the Black position were reduced to Justice Douglas and to Black himself. Even those two have differed over the relevance of the argument in particular cases involving the protection of accused persons.[51] It is doubtful whether any of the recent appointees will adhere to the Black position.[52] Currently, at any rate, constitutional restrictions on state action are to be measured not by the language of the first eight amendments but by the language of the Fourteenth Amendment, and particularly by the Supreme Court's interpretation of the due process clause, the fluctuations of which so deeply disturb Justice Black.

5 If the constitutional theory advanced by Justice Black has not been well received, Justice Frankfurter has also had difficulty in presenting his own theory of due process in a clear and acceptable fashion. Faced with the implied accusation of expanding or contracting due process depending on whether he wanted to restrict state action or leave it free, he has asserted again and again a doctrine of self-denial on the part of the Court. His doctrine sounds much like that of Justice Stone, save that Stone was apt to be self-denying with respect to property rights and not where protection of personal rights was involved, whereas Frankfurter in practice as well as theory rejected the concept of "preferred position." In the year following the Adamson decision he attempted to expound in *Haley v. Ohio* the correct method of finding the content of due process. Subtle and elusive as were its criteria, the Court could not escape the duty of judicial review. Yet the nature of the duty required humility.

> Humility in this context means an alert self-scrutiny so as to avoid infusing into the vagueness of a constitutional command one's merely private notions. Like other mortals, judges, though unaware, may be in the grip of prepossessions. The only way to relax such a grip, the only way to avoid finding in the Constitution the personal bias one has placed in it, is to explore the influences that have shaped one's unanalyzed views in order to lay bare prepossessions.[53]

Essentially, he thought, the task of applying due process in a criminal case, in an instance of alleged coerced confession, invited psychological judgment, "a psychological judgment that reflects deep, even if inarticulate, feelings of our society,"[54] a judgment that called for resort to all the relevant evidence. But how was this to be done?

> The answer, as has already been intimated, depends on an evaluation of psychological factors, or, more accurately stated, upon the pervasive feelings of society regarding such psychological factors. Unfortunately, we cannot draw upon any formulated expression of the existence of such feelings. Nor are there available experts on such matters to guide the judicial judg-

> ment. Our constitutional system makes it the Court's duty to interpret those feelings of society to which the due process clause gives legal protection. Because of their inherent vagueness the tests by which we are to be guided are most unsatisfactory, but such as they are we must apply them.[55]

As if sensing the fact that his position was not fully understood, or at any rate that it needed further elucidation, he restated it in a later case:

> Due process is that which comports with the deepest notions of what is fair and right and just. The more fundamental the beliefs are the less likely they are to be explicitly stated. But respect for them is of the very essence of the due process clause. In enforcing them this Court does not translate personal views into constitutional limitations. In applying such a large, untechnical concept as "due process," the Court enforces those permanent and pervasive feelings of our society as to which there is compelling evidence of the kind relevant to judgments on our social institutions.[56]

Yet in spite of the restatement, Justice Frankfurter's position remained hauntingly if intriguingly unclear. He was not measuring due process by the whims of the moment, no matter how widely held. He was not thinking of a content that could be measured by public opinion polls. He did not deem prerequisite an interpretation of due process spelled out in a constitution or other public document. He may have had in mind, indeed, something approximating Rousseau's "general will," which was not merely the active and conscious will of the majority, or perhaps even of all the people, but underlay premises so deep that their holders might not be conscious of their existence and might not be able to reflect them in any calculated expression. If this was true, he was asking justices to perform a herculean task. They must not only divest themselves of personal prepossessions of which they might not be aware, but they must also peer into society for still deeper, and in some sense universal, prepossessions about which particular individuals were ignorant as far as their conscious minds were concerned, or at any rate were likely to be inarticulate.

So difficult was the task of interpreting due process as here defined that even the justices who may have agreed with Justice Frankfurter's analysis had difficulty in applying it in other cases. In *Wolf v. Colorado,* Justice Frankfurter resorted to what under the circumstances was a barbed statement:

> The notion that the "due process of law" guaranteed by the Fourteenth Amendment is shorthand for the first eight amendments of the Constitution and thereby incorporates them has been rejected by this Court again and again, after impressive consideration.[57]

Speaking for the Supreme Court, he permitted a Colorado court to convict an abortionist on the basis of evidence seized without a warrant under circumstances that, he said, would have violated the Fourth Amendment had the trial been held in a federal court. Three justices dissented.

On the other hand, Justice Frankfurter spoke for the Court in *Rochin v. California,* in which, on the basis of due process, a state decision that upheld conviction for possession of narcotics was reversed on the basis of evidence vomited up by the defendant after he was forcibly given an emetic. Due process, Frankfurter contended, was not to be derided as a resort to a revival of natural law. The content of due process could not be frozen at some fixed stage of time or thought. Each case required evaluation in the light of all the relevant factors. In the present case,

> This is conduct that shocks the conscience. Illegally breaking into the privacy of the petitioner, the struggle to open his mouth and remove what was there, the forcible extraction of his stomach's contents—this course of proceeding by agents of government to obtain evidence is bound to offend even hardened sensibilities. They are methods too close to the rack and the screw to permit of constitutional differentiation.[58]

The two writers of concurring opinions preferred the Black formula to Frankfurter's due process formula.

In the Wolf case use of evidence obtained by deplorable conduct of state officials was not held to violate due process, while in the Rochin case due process was found to be denied.

Real distinctions are here apparent even to the layman. It is one thing to enter without a warrant the office of a doctor and search his papers for evidence of the crime of abortion and to use the discovered evidence against him in a criminal case; it is another thing to invade a man's room and to use violence to extract the contents of his stomach in order to use those contents as evidence. But intermediate cases were sure to appear in which neither the precedents nor Justice Frankfurter's expositions of due process would lead clearly to decision. *Irvine v. California* was such an intermediate case. There the state sought evidence of illegal gambling by a man who was believed to be a professional gambler. State police made a key to the front door of his home, entered when all members of the family were absent, and installed a microphone in the bedroom. "The police devised means to hear every word that was said in the Irvine household for more than a month." [59] The relevant conversations were used to convict of a crime.

Justice Frankfurter, adhering to his position that "a state cannot resort to methods that offend civilized standards of decency and fairness," [60] contended that the malodorous conduct of the police vitiated the use of the evidence they had collected—that such use in court violated due process. Only Justice Burton agreed with him, though two other justices voted for reversal of the judgment on other grounds. The five majority justices, on the other hand, classified the Irvine case with the Wolf case and affirmed the judgment, but they were unable to agree on an opinion that could be listed as the "opinion of the Court." Justice Clark, who spoke only for himself and who voted with the majority only because he regarded the Wolf case as a binding precedent, noted: "In truth, the practical result of this ad hoc approach is simply that when five justices are sufficiently revolted by local police action, a conviction is overturned and a guilty man may go free." [61]

So it is that due process with respect to personal rights, for all its definiteness at its core, became so indefinite at its periphery that no amount of eloquent and perceptive analysis provided much guidance for citizens or government officers or even members of the Supreme Court. In this respect there was difference only in degree from due process as a protection of property. In the latter field Justice Douglas could say for a unanimous Court in 1955:

> The day is gone when this Court uses the due process clause of the Fourteenth Amendment to strike down state laws, regulatory of business and industrial conditions, because they may be unwise, improvident, or out of harmony with a particular school of thought.[62]

Members of the Court in earlier years, when property received more careful protection, would of course have contended that they never struck down state laws for the reasons mentioned by Justice Douglas—that they struck laws down only because they were unconstitutional. In varying degree the Frankfurter explanation of the nature of due process might have been acceptable to these earlier justices, who regarded property as the cornerstone of our constitutional system, but their conception of the sentiments of the people, or of the "general will," or of the laws of the Supreme Being, would have been very different from those of the justices of the Court in the modern era.

With current justices as with their predecessors, it continues to be true that the distinctions of the law are primarily distinctions of degree. Although in the case above mentioned Justice Douglas revived a long-unpopular quotation from Chief Justice Waite in *Munn v. Illinois* to the effect that "For protection against abuses by legislatures the people must resort to the polls and not to the courts," we do not reasonably infer that due process would never be used to curb legislative invasion of property rights. It is rather because the present degree of regulation is close enough to a pattern deemed generally acceptable that the courts are willing to permit evils to be eliminated gradually through the political process rather than intervene when called upon to do so in exercise of their restrictive power under the due process clause. It seems quite clear, for example, that a state which set out to expropriate a privately owned transportation system or to compel it to serve the public without compensation would find itself stopped in short order. With respect to property rights the Supreme Court has abandoned the lines of argument along which protection was once afforded, but there is no reason for assuming that it has abdicated altogether.

6 This discussion began with a summary of constitutional prohibitions laid upon federal and state governments and proceeded to illustrate Supreme Court performance in applying these prohibitions by an account of its experience with due process of law. Its performance in connection with other prohibitions is highly similar. We may illustrate this briefly in terms of equal protection of the laws, which the states are forbidden to deny, and unreasonable searches and seizures, which are forbidden to the federal government.

It is common knowledge that the equal protection clause was enacted primarily for the purpose of protecting the rights of Negroes—a topic that will be discussed at greater length elsewhere. Its wider application, however, permeates the whole field of state activity, and its guarantee of equal protection has been held to encompass the "protection of equal laws." [63] Yet the human pattern is so diverse that it is quite impossible in some circumstances, and not feasible in others, to treat all people and all situations alike. As a result, whether in connection with taxation or police power activity, it has been necessary to group people and situations by classes and to insist merely that all classes be treated alike—with endless controversy over the legitimacy of particular classifications. A few cases tell the story as far as current or recent members of the Supreme Court are concerned.

One of these cases, *Goesaert v. Cleary*, which the justices were able to handle with a touch of humor, involved a Michigan statute forbidding the licensing of women as bartenders, with the exception of those who were the wives or daughters of male owners of liquor establishments. The plaintiffs claimed that they were denied equal protection of the laws by the discrimination in favor of the wives and daughters of male owners. Justice Frankfurter, for a majority of the Court, rejected this contention. Michigan could forbid all women from working behind a bar.

> This is so despite the vast changes in the social and legal position of women. The fact that women may now have achieved the virtues that men have long claimed as their prerogatives and now indulge in vices that men have long practiced, does not preclude the states from drawing a sharp line between the sexes, certainly in such matters as regulation of the liquor traffic.[64]

While under the equal protection clause a state could not engage in irrational discrimination, the Court could not override Michigan's assumption that "the oversight assured through ownership of a bar by a barmaid's husband or father minimizes hazards that may confront a barmaid without such protecting oversight." [65] Three dissenting justices argued that while the equal protection clause did not require "abstract symmetry," it did forbid the discrimination here, which drew a line between the daughter of a male owner and the female owner or her daughter, who might have provided for sufficient male protection. The differences among the justices were of the same intangibility as those involved in the interpretation of due process of law.

A state may forbid professional advertising by dentists without forbidding it to chiropodists and other professionals.[66] It may exclude from its streets vehicles advertising businesses other than those they are operated in, while permitting the owners' advertising to be displayed on delivery trucks.[67] It may apply antitrust laws to industry but exclude agriculture.[68] It may require prescriptions for glasses fitted to the eyes, even for replacement of broken ones, and forbid advertising of the business, but exempt from such restrictions the sale of ready-to-wear glasses.[69] When the Court accepts a discriminating classification, as in these instances, it shows deference to the judgment of the legislature. Yet, as in the instance of due process, it may find the classification so offensive that it will reject the state determination as unconstitutional. In those instances, as in the race cases to be discussed later, it considers the nature of constitutional purpose and intent. Here again there is a central core of judicial agreement but a surrounding area of haze in which judges find it easy to disagree.

Likewise illustrative of the enforcement of constitutional prohibitions are the cases resting on the Fourth Amendment, which forbids the federal government to make unreasonable searches and seizures and requires that warrants for searches or arrest be issued only upon probable cause and with the support of oath or affirmation. Under the amendment it is well settled that federal officers may not make arrests on the basis of whims or unverified suspicions and may not at will violate private premises. Yet the amendment was not intended to require absolute proof of guilt before an arrest or a search could be made. In cases decided over many years the Supreme Court has been drawing the line between the permissible and the forbidden, often with sharp differences among the members. In this field as in others, some of the stormiest disagreements came from the Roosevelt-Truman Court. A few examples will illustrate this.

In 1947, in *Harris v. United States*,[70] the Supreme Court in a five-to-four decision upheld the seizure and use of evidence of violation of a federal statute, although the seizure took place while the defendant was being held under arrest, not for violating that statute but an entirely different one. In other words, on the face of the record it was pure luck that federal officers found the evidence they did find while searching for evidence of a different crime. There being no search warrant, the search was justified only by the rule that a search may be made without a warrant in the immediate vicinity of a person who is being held under a warrant of arrest; yet there was no proper relation between the arrest and the evidence that was found and used to win a conviction. Four justices protested in three indignant dissenting opinions.

In 1948 the balance shifted the other way. In *Trupiano v.*

United States[71] the Court in a five-to-four decision set aside a conviction based on evidence of operating a still that was gathered without a search warrant at the time of arresting the defendant in the vicinity of the still. The four dissenters thought that denial of the right to use the evidence ran counter to a long line of precedents.

In 1950 the balance shifted again. In *United States v. Rabinowitz,*[72] by a vote of five to three with one justice not sitting, the Court overruled the Trupiano decision and permitted use of evidence collected by searching without a warrant the business premises of a man held in the premises during the search pursuant to an arrest made with a valid warrant of arrest. The three cases were not exactly alike—cases never are—but they were similar enough as to facts to indicate complete discontinuity on the part of the Supreme Court. It seems clear that the second shift in position resulted primarily from changes in Court personnel. Even today we cannot be sure that a settled position has been established on the periphery of this constitutional prohibition.

The extent of the search-and-seizure prohibition has peculiar importance for the American people today because of the development of new instruments for picking up and recording sound and for disclosing what is intended to be private. It is becoming increasingly difficult to be sure that any conversation is out of the range of some listening or recording instrument. The Supreme Court has long been keenly aware of the implied legal difficulty. As long ago as 1928 it held, though only by a five-to-four vote, that accumulation of evidence by tapping telephone wires off the premises of the accused did not violate the Fourth Amendment.[73] In 1942 it held that the amendment was not violated by the accumulation of evidence through use of a detectaphone for listening through a wall to a conversation in another room.[74] Here only one justice dissented, but two others expressed the wish that the Court overrule the wiretapping case and eliminate it as a precedent.

The full implications of the use of modern instruments became apparent in 1952 in *On Lee v. United States.* On Lee, the operator of a laundry, was convicted of the illegal sale of opium. Part of the evidence against On Lee was collected through the use of Chin Poy, a former employee, as an undercover agent or "stool pigeon" of the Bureau of Narcotics. Chin Poy entered the laundry and engaged On Lee in conversation apparently inaudible to anyone else, and secured damaging admissions from him. Unknown to On Lee, Chin Poy carried a concealed microphone from which sound was transmitted to a receiving set held by another agent outside the building. The admissions were used to secure the conviction.

The Supreme Court upheld the conviction by a vote of five to four. The majority held that there was no unlawful search or seizure. Said Justice Jackson:

> The use of bifocals, field glasses or the telescope to magnify the object of a witness' vision is not a forbidden search or seizure, even if they focus without his knowledge or consent upon what one supposes to be private indiscretions. It would be a dubious service to the genuine liberties protected by the Fourth Amendment to make them bedfellows with spurious liberties improvised by farfetched analogies which would liken eavesdropping on a conversation, with the connivance of one of the parties, to an unreasonable search or seizure.[75]

Justice Burton, on the other hand, as one of the four dissenters, soberly noted:

> In this case the words were picked up without warrant or consent *within* the constitutionally inviolate "house" of a person entitled to protection there against unreasonable searches and seizures of his person, house, papers and effects. It is inevitable that the line be narrow between, on the one hand, the constitutional right of a person to be free from unreasonable searches and seizures and, on the other, the need for effective prosecution of crime. Drawing the line is a continuing process. The important thing is that the direction of the line that emerges from successive cases be clear.[76]

The case illustrates the delicacy of the judicial task, and closely resembles the type of performance called for in the application of due process and other constitutional concepts. Similar responsibilities are involved when the Court must define the limits of the privilege of the writ of habeas corpus, the area covered by ex post facto laws and bills of attainder, the extent of the political privilege where race is involved, and the other areas of constitutional limitation.

7 It is true, as stated above, that the constitutional provisions here under discussion, whether due process, equal protection, search and seizure, or the many other provisions briefly mentioned, are purely negations. They do not give power to any agency. Even the power to make these negations effective comes from other provisions in the Constitution and from implications therefrom. Yet as negations they fulfill their intended function of limiting the outward drive of the dynamics of government. They protect the social order against the abuse of governmental power, they purify the operations of government so that the legitimate purposes of government may be fulfilled. Yet concepts of legitimacy change along with changes in the areas to which constitutional prohibitions are to be applied. The constitutional language is old but the applications are new, if not in their entirety nevertheless sufficiently to create doubt and to require rationalization by the Court. The process results in judicial stress and strain, even though it is stress and strain over the interpretation of constitutional negations. The positives and the negatives, indeed, become so involved that examination often fails to disclose whether the Court is primarily concerned with the prohibitions that are written into the Constitution or with the limits that, quite apart from specific prohibitions, are inherent in the positive powers themselves.

It is worth restating that, whether judicial preoccupation is primarily with positive or negative constitutional provisions, the function of the Supreme Court is predominantly negative. Where governmental action is concerned, the options of the Court are limited: it may merely refrain from interference with what government wants to do, or it may hold such action either unauthorized or forbidden by the Constitution. It cannot propose and initiate alternative programs. Yet out of this pattern of essential negation develops a judicial function that is worthy of important mention and that is in itself positive. Whether in the process of stopping government action or refusing to stop it, the Court rationalizes its decisions in terms of the constitutional pattern as a whole, or at any rate in terms of some considerable segment of that pattern. It articulates the character of the constitutional system and indicates the nature of its unity. Along broad lines the Court is a rationalizing and synthesizing agency, and in this sense its work has value far beyond the range of the settlement of individual disputes. Congress, in the enactment of statutes, operates piecemeal. It deals with fragments of situations. It reflects the critical needs in particular situations and the political drives of the moment rather than the broad pattern of governmental activity. It seldom takes time to relate one segment of activity to another. The same is true of the mass of activities in the executive branch. The multiple hands of government operate with little awareness of one another's doings. Even the President, as the head of that branch, seldom succeeds in rationalizing it into a unity—seldom makes an effort to do so. He too is under the pressures of the moment. He speaks with an eye to immediate response and to such factors as the impact of what he might say on international relations at the moment. But the Supreme Court has at least a greater degree of aloofness, greater opportunity for achieving objectivity, and it has as part of its equipment the tradition of the unity of the law. More than the other branches of the government, it is in a position to explain and justify, and thereby to promote, the cohesiveness of our people under our constitutional system. It is primarily because of this opportunity and this capacity that the attention here given to the Court is justified. For further illustration we shall turn now to the work of the Court in relation to our basic national loyalties, or rather to its handling of cases in which loyalty has been at least allegedly threatened by subversion—subversion that might destroy the nation itself.

III *The Threat of Subversion*

The threat of subversion, so much discussed in the United States since the beginning of World War II and particularly during the "cold war" with the Communist nations, is a phenomenon known to all groups that have a sense of their own organic importance. However great may be the ideal of tolerance and brotherhood, physical attack or attack upon the ideology of the group brings defensive action that may go all the way to the stage of defensive warfare. An extreme example in European history was resort by the Christian church to the tortures of the Inquisition to protect the institution that was founded to propagate a gospel of love. The spiritual end was held to justify the physical means. The organic theories of the state propagated by Fascist and Nazi doctrines, presenting the state as the supreme organism, easily justified the repression of dissent in act or word or even in thought—even, indeed, the kind of dissent involved in being born a member of some other than the master race. The Soviet Union's policy of ruthless repression of dissenting acts, words, and beliefs is of the same pattern. In each of these examples, extreme emphasis has been put on the organic character of the group and on the prime importance of its doctrine, with little or no room left for individual dissent or uniqueness.

American tradition has tended to underplay the requirement of conformity and to maximize the freedom of the individual within the national group. The new continent with its vast expanse and seemingly unlimited resources drew from the Old World immigrants who sought escape from religious, social, or political coercion and who believed in the value of individual variety. They and their descendants framed a Constitution "to secure the blessings of liberty to ourselves and our posterity." Yet for us as for other groups, the threat of disintegrating attack has brought coercion to conform. We fought a Civil War to prevent the splitting of the Union. The Copperheads of the Civil War period, the pro-Germans and "slackers" of World War I, and the "fifth columnists" of World War II were legitimate objects of repressive measures. Radical doctrines of the past three quarters of a century spread by anarchists, syndicalists, socialists, Bolsheviks, and Communists have given rise to many kinds of governmental restrictions.

So it is that, in spite of our tradition of liberty and individualism, threats to our basic beliefs and our internal cohesion have brought the curbing of individual liberty and the liberty of dissenting factions in the interest of the welfare of the group as seen by its dominant elements. From the point of view of a justification of the coercive aspect of our behavior we have not been deeply philosophical. This is not to say that we have philosophized like libertarians and behaved like totalitarians. By comparison with most other social orders we have maintained a high degree of individual liberty. But with regard to the internal coercion in which we have engaged, we have worked out no adequate philosophy beyond a generalized commitment to democracy and majority rule. Rather, we have tended to deal with coercion as an exceptional area, as an area that is sufficiently identified by labeling it as the exception to the rule that liberty shall prevail. We talk little about the alleged organic oneness of the American people, save as it is necessary for us to stand as one against some foreign enemy. Here we exercise coercion not primarily to serve the welfare of the nation as a nation, but rather to promote the welfare of the individuals whom the nation exists to serve. Yet amid the tensions of actual warfare or of prolonged readiness for possible attack, we tend to lose sight of the individual and to personalize the nation and to make national loyalty a paramount requirement.

Under these circumstances the Supreme Court, if it speaks at all, is required either to flout the contemporary demand for coercion or to adduce a body of organic theory that has no adequate rootage in our traditions. It is not surprising that the dilemma puts the Court under strain or that in writing opinions the justices scatter far and wide in their interpretations of constitutional law. Because it touches deep emotions, the story of the Court's dealings with subversion has been told and retold many times from many points of view. Some of us are already tired of hearing it. Yet it is like a recording that, for all our weariness, must be replayed again and again for nuances as yet unheard or not fully appreciated. Such is the justification for retelling the story here.

1 During the past two decades, questions of loyalty to the United States and controversies over subversive activities have more heavily preoccupied the Supreme Court than during all the earlier decades of American history. Cases have dealt with matters all the way from treason, the grossest of offenses to be committed against the nation, through espionage and sedition, to attitudes of disloyalty that might make in-

dividuals unfit for government employment, or for employment in industries producing goods for government use, or for service as officers of labor unions. Preoccupation with national loyalty, or with subversion, taking the latter term to imply the breakdown of loyalty and an effort to undermine the nation, is not the product of any sudden decadence to befall the United States. It is the product rather of the shattering of illusions about our physical isolation from the rest of the world and our invulnerability to destroying attack. As the Supreme Court suggested in the Cramer case in 1945, "We have managed to do without treason prosecutions to a degree that probably would be impossible except while a people was singularly confident of external security and internal stability." [1] The same is true about lesser offenses related to loyalty and national security. The end, with World War I, of a century of relatively comfortable isolation and assumed invulnerability from foreign attack, and the discovery, with World War II, that world conflict was something which could happen again and was not merely the product of the rapacity of munitions makers and bankers seeking profit, drove us to a sudden search for defenses in a condition of horribly dangerous vulnerability. The result was great stress and strain not only in the Supreme Court but in all branches of government and among the people generally.

Our task, therefore, has been that of refurbishing old instruments and developing new ones to deal with old and new methods of subversion and to bolster up the protections that derive from wholehearted and self-denying loyalty. We feared betrayal in such various forms as the sabotage of industrial plants, the fomenting of strikes in plants producing for war purposes, the disclosure of military and industrial secrets to enemies or potential enemies, and less tangible threats that led in 1944 to the indirectly expressed attitude that there was something slightly unpatriotic in not supporting Franklin D. Roosevelt for re-election—which had its parallel in 1956 in a similar feeling about the re-election of Dwight D. Eisenhower.

Whether dealing with treason or with some lesser aspect

of subversion, the Roosevelt-Truman Supreme Court found the issues difficult, and the justices divided sharply in this field as in many others. It is easiest to begin with the discussion of treason, which has the unique distinction of being the one crime defined in the Constitution and of being hedged about with special provisions as to proof of the offense. Article III, Section 3, provides:

> Treason against the United States shall consist only in levying war against them, or in adhering to their enemies, giving them aid and comfort. No person shall be convicted of treason unless on the testimony of two witnesses to the same overt act, or on confession in open court.

As discussed in the Cramer case, mentioned above, and in authoritative analyses of the subject,[2] the very name of treason vibrates with emotion, and our English forebears had long known the extent of its possible abuse. Treason in England was of course an offense against the sovereign, who in a monarchy is much easier to identify than in a republic. Except as they were curbed by the restrictions gradually built into English law, the king and those who spoke in his name could easily impute treachery to, and apply the severe punishment for treason against, any who had the temerity to differ with the constituted authorities. It was possible to get convictions without the evidence that humane standards would require for such a serious offense.

The framers of the Constitution knew of the historical abuses, and they had had immediate experience with treason in connection with the American Revolution. In a sense, indeed, all of them were themselves guilty of treason under English law, having levied war against their king or given aid and comfort to the rebellion. But they had also seen excesses in the American states in punishing traitors to the states or to the newly established Union—traitors who were called such because they refused to be traitors to the king and who, indeed, are known to history by the name of Loyalists. It was with this background that the framers limited treason in the constitutional definition and required for conviction the testimony of two witnesses to the same overt act or confession in open court.

Since disloyalty to a country is never completely eradicated and since the United States has been many times at war, it is surprising that the nation has never put any person to death for the crime of treason. The death penalty for Julius and Ethel Rosenberg, which was enforced in 1953, was not for treason but for conspiracy to violate the Espionage Act of 1917.[3] The absence of convictions of treason with supreme penalties has no doubt resulted from many causes. The crime carries a stigma that juries hesitate to attach except when emotions are most overheated, and when the record shows convictions in such emotional situations, executives are inclined to commute sentences or to issue pardons. Furthermore, it may be easier, when dealing with the type of conduct involved in accusations of treason, to get convictions for sedition or espionage or other offenses, which may or may not have lesser official penalties—as witness the execution of the Rosenbergs.

It is also surprising that, with one exception, no treason cases were decided by the Supreme Court prior to the 1940's. The exception was the Bollman and Swartwout case of 1807, in which Chief Justice Marshall held that treason in the form of levying war did not exist unless there had been an actual assemblage of persons for the achievement of a treasonable purpose.[4] True, members of the Court were not unfamiliar with the law of treason. Justice James Wilson had participated as counsel in treason cases and probably did much work on the drafting of the constitutional clause.[5] Many of the justices participated in treason cases in their capacity as circuit judges, as did Chief Justice Marshall in the trial of Aaron Burr—to give an outstanding example.[6]

With wholesale disloyalty in the form of secession and civil war, it might have been expected that treason trials would occur in large numbers and that many offenders would pay extreme penalties—for here war to the full was levied against the United States, and there was no lack of witnesses of overt acts. But here again humanitarian sentiment intervened. Northern residents were willing to fight against the South but not to convict Southern warriors of treason, with its stigma and its possible death penalty. To prevent the blocking of all punishment by unwilling juries, Congress in 1862 restricted the punishment of treason, when it consisted in giving aid and comfort to, or engaging in, an insurrection against the United States, to ten years' imprisonment or a fine of ten thousand dollars, or both.[7] Some convictions took place under the amended statute, but some judges, including Chief Justice Taney, convinced that a fair and impartial trial of persons accused of treason was not possible in the emotionalized atmosphere of the war, continued the cases from term to term until the war was over, after which they were dropped without trial.[8] Not even the leaders of the rebellion were tried for levying war against the United States.

During World War I little use was made of the treason statute for punishment of disloyalty. Instead, the government proceeded on the basis of newly enacted statutes punishing for espionage, sedition, and sabotage, offenses that will be discussed later but for which, it may be said briefly here, convictions could be secured on the basis of circumstantial evidence and without the requirement of two witnesses to the same overt act. Resort to the treason statute in cases that were appealed to the Supreme Court came during World War II, after the Court had upheld the trial by military commission of members of the German armed forces who had landed in secret on American shores from submarines, dressed themselves in civilian clothes, and then gone about the business of planning the sabotage of American war production and in other ways interfering with the war effort.[9] These invaders were tried not for treason but for violation of the law of war and the Articles of War, and they received the death penalty. The civil cases that reached the Supreme Court had to do with the offenses of native Americans and naturalized citizens of German origin, who had aided and protected, or, in the language of the Constitution and the statute, "comforted" the invaders.

The two civil offenders whose convictions were passed upon by the Supreme Court were sentenced to fines and imprisonment. The Court reversed one conviction and upheld the other, providing in the several opinions the first elaborate discussion of the law of treason to come from the Supreme Court, with the exception of the John Marshall opinion in the Bollman and Swartwout case mentioned above. In *Cramer v. United States* [10] the Court reversed the judgment of conviction of Andrew Cramer, who had been accused of giving aid and comfort to Werner Thiel, one of the saboteurs. In terms of a statement of acts too complicated for summary here, it had been proved that Cramer associated extensively with Thiel and had taken care of a considerable sum of money for him—money that had been provided by the German government for purposes of sabotage. More than the requisite number of two witnesses were available. Yet the Supreme Court, speaking through Justice Jackson, was unable to get the necessary linkage between treasonable intent, individual overt acts as testified to by two witnesses, and a chain of treasonable conduct such that the conviction could stand in the light of the constitutional requirements.

The overturning of Cramer's conviction created the widespread belief that it would be next to impossible under any circumstances to obtain a conviction for treason that the Supreme Court would sustain. Indeed, an indignant minority of four justices, speaking through Justice Douglas, implied that the majority had inadequately stated the relevant facts in the process of reversing the judgment of conviction:

> The opinion of the Court is written on a hypothetical state of facts, not on the facts presented by the record. It states a rule of law based on an interpretation of the Constitution which is not only untenable but which is also unnecessary for the decision. It overlooks the basic issue on which our disposition of the case must turn. In order to reach that issue we must have a more exact appreciation of the facts than can be gleaned from the opinion of the Court.[11]

Justice Douglas then proceeded to state the facts for the minority in such a way as to show that treason had been proved.

Willard Hurst, of the University of Wisconsin Law School, who had compiled for the Department of Justice in the Cramer case, and for insertion in the appendix to its brief, a detailed history of treason in English and American law, wrote indignantly in the *Harvard Law Review* that the majority opinion "in its efforts to develop the implications of the constitutional definition of the crime, either invented some bad law or added confusion to an already muddled subject." [12]

Yet the Court, voting eight to one, did uphold the conviction of Hans Max Haupt, who was accused of sheltering his son, Herbert Haupt, another of the saboteurs, and of getting his son a job in a plant engaged in war production and helping him to buy an automobile, with the treasonable intent to aid his son in his criminal purpose. Dealing with the point on which Justice Murphy was to dissent, Justice Jackson, again speaking for the Court, referred to the argument that the defendant "merely had the misfortune to sire a traitor and all he did was to act as an indulgent father toward a disloyal son." [13] But it was permissible for the jury to decide, as it had presumably done from evidence of the father's conduct, that

> The son had the misfortune of being a chip off the old block—a tree inclined as the twig had been bent—metaphors which express the common sense observation that parents are as likely to influence the character of their children as are children to shape that of their parents.[14]

As was perhaps to be expected, Justice Douglas, who had written a dissenting opinion in the Cramer case, wrote a concurring opinion in the Haupt case to show that the two cases were really very much alike and that the Court in affirming the judgment of conviction in the Haupt case was now properly returning to a correct interpretation of the law. However that may be, the two cases further demonstrated the great difficulty of determining when treasonable acts have been committed and of following the trial procedures prescribed by the Constitution.

World War II brought to the Supreme Court another treason case, that of Tomoya Kawakita, an American-born citizen of Japanese ancestry, who by virtue of that ancestry and Japanese law could claim Japanese nationality as well. Using an American passport, Kawakita was visiting in Japan at the time of the outbreak of the war. As a man with dual nationality, Kawakita did not invite American prosecution for treason merely by the act of working for a Japanese war industry. His treasonable conduct lay in acts of violence against American prisoners of war in Japan for whom he had acted as interpreter—"acts of hostility toward this country which he was not required by Japan to perform." [15] When Japan lost the war he returned to the United States as an American citizen. He was recognized by victims of his brutal treatment and was tried for treason. The government had no difficulty in proving overt acts of treason by two witnesses, but had to meet the contention that Kawakita had expatriated himself from the United States and therefore could not, while residing in the country of his Japanese nationality, be guilty of treason against the United States. With three justices dissenting and two others not sitting, the Supreme Court held that he had not expatriated himself, and that the judgment of conviction for treason must be affirmed. In effect the Court seemed to be saying that a man could not play cat-and-mouse with his American citizenship, dropping it when it seemed unattractive, picking it up again for return to the United States, and again discarding it when it became a basis for a prosecution for treason.

Although other trials for treason took place during and after the war, and some convictions were secured, it could still be said in 1945:

> There have been less than three score treason prosecutions pressed to trial by the federal government; there has been no execution on a federal treason conviction; and the Executive

has commonly intervened to pardon, or at least mitigate the sentence of those convicted.[16]

2 The threescore prosecutions for treason represent but a small fraction of the total number of cases involving charges of various degrees of subversion. What has happened has been the development of other categories of crime that at once carry a lesser stigma than that of treason and are free of the rigid requirements for conviction that attach to treason cases. There is no evidence that the framers of the Constitution intended by the treason clause to prevent the punishment of subversive conduct less offensive than treason or to impose the requirement of two witnesses to the same overt act or confession in open court as conditions of such punishment. Our concern here is with the degree of punishment of such lesser offenses, with the possible extraction of treasonable content for classification under other titles so that convictions could be more easily secured, and with the application of penalties that might be no less than the penalties actually exacted in connection with the few treason convictions that have been won. Or rather, our concern is with the conduct of the Supreme Court in connection with these developments.

Congress reached out to punish such lesser offenses as early as 1798, when in the so-called Sedition Act it provided fine and imprisonment not only for combinations to obstruct enforcement of the laws but for any person who

> shall write, print, utter or publish, or shall cause or procure to be written, printed, uttered or published, or shall knowingly and willingly assist or aid in writing, printing, uttering or publishing any false, scandalous and malicious writing or writings against the government of the United States, or the President of the United States, with the intent to defame the said government, or either house of the said Congress, or the said President, or to bring them, or either of them into contempt or disrepute; or to excite against them, or either or any of them, the hatred of the good people of the United States, or to excite any unlawful combinations therein, for opposing or resisting any law of the United States, or any act of the President of the United States, done in pursuance of any such law, or of

> the powers in him vested by the Constitution of the United States. . . .[17]

Although the statute was not re-enacted at its expiration in 1801, and the United States, in the language of Justice Holmes, showed its repentance for the measure by repaying the fines imposed,[18] this early sedition measure set a pattern for later enactment of measures for dealing with subversion short of treason.

During World War I Congress enacted a measure known as the Espionage Act with a wide variety of provisions and with penalties ranging from fine and imprisonment to death. It enacted an amendment thereto known as the Sedition Act, and an independent measure known as the Sabotage Act. These measures gave rise to a wide range of prosecutions for subversive conduct. Nowhere was the legislation seriously challenged on the ground that in this field only conduct on the level of treason could be forbidden or that the conduct described bore the taint of treason and so could be punished only as treason and pursuant to the provisions of the treason clause of the Constitution. The challenges were made, rather, in terms of the freedoms of speech, press, and assembly protected by the First Amendment. In prosecutions for treason, convictions could be secured only if overt acts were proved. In prosecutions for espionage and sedition, on the other hand, the only acts involved might be in the form of speech or publication or assembly, which the federal government could prohibit only by dragging them from their First Amendment shelter. Most of the important cases arising under these war statutes, indeed, had to do with attempts to discourage enlistment and to lower morale in the armed services. They were activities primarily of speech and publication.

The story of the war cases and the announcement and continued development of the clear and present danger doctrine marks one of the most exhaustively studied phases of American history, one that can be presented here only in capsule form. The first statement came in *Schenck v. United States*, where Justice Holmes spoke for a unanimous Court. In many places and in ordinary times, Justice Holmes admitted, the defendants would have been within their constitutional rights in saying all that was said in the circular which gave rise to their prosecution. But the character of every act depends on the circumstances under which it was done. "The most stringent protection of free speech would not protect a man in falsely shouting fire in a theater, and causing a panic." [19] He then attempted, in language that has been quoted again and again, to delineate the principle for measuring constitutional freedom of speech in given instances:

> The question in every case is whether the words used are used in such circumstances and are of such a nature as to create a clear and present danger that they will bring about the substantive evils that Congress has a right to prevent. It is a question of proximity and degree. When a nation is at war many things that might be said in time of peace are such a hindrance to its effort that their utterance will not be endured so long as men fight, and that no court could regard them as protected by any constitutional right.[20]

In his recent study of Justices Holmes and Brandeis, Samuel J. Konefsky deals at length with the clear and present danger cases and with scholarly comments on the development of the doctrine. He finds that Justice Holmes was "not primarily concerned with propounding a new test of constitutionality," [21] that the concept "did not emerge as possessing any clear-cut meaning or content," [22] and that Justice Brandeis "took the theory much more seriously than did Holmes." [23] Justice Brandeis characterized the clear and present danger doctrine as a "rule of reason." Correctly applied, he contended, it would "preserve the right of free speech both from suppression by tyrannous, well-meaning majorities, and from abuse by irresponsible, fanatical minorities." [24]

In the Dennis case, to be discussed hereafter, Justice Jackson noted that the doctrine had been denounced by Alexander Meiklejohn on the ground that it "annuls the most significant purpose of the First Amendment," [25] and praised by Zechariah Chafee, Jr., as giving "for the first time an authoritative judicial interpretation in accordance with the purposes of the Constitution." [26] Justice Jackson agreed that the Holmes statement was the only original thought on the subject, adding, "All agree that it means something very important, but no two seem to agree on what it is." [27] Justice Frankfurter characterized the doctrine as a "felicitous phrase" [28] and as a "literary phrase," [29] and warned against taking it out of context for use in other areas.

What seems to have happened was that Justice Holmes, who had a flair for colorful phraseology, announced the clear and present danger doctrine when speaking for the Supreme Court in a case in which all justices found sufficient danger to justify the control of speech. In all probability his colleagues gave little thought to the phraseology at the time the words were written into the opinion. Other cases followed in which all members likewise agreed that the danger was great enough to justify control. Then the Court began to divide. Justices Holmes and Brandeis began to dissent against decisions upholding control and to contend that a clear and present danger did not exist in the cases at hand. The majority, instead of talking about clear and present danger, left that concept to the minority and talked about bad tendency, or manifest tendency to bring about preventable evils, as in the Gitlow case of 1925.[30]

The clear and present danger doctrine, therefore, became for a time primarily an instrument of judicial liberalism, whatever the interpretation given to the doctrine, with rejection only by those liberals who, like Alexander Meiklejohn, contended that First Amendment rights were absolute, were subject to no limitation whatsoever. But gradually, as liberalism in terms of the Holmes-Brandeis heritage became dominant on the Court, the heirs of the founders of the doctrine became involved in controversy over its meaning. Operating in a field far from that of military danger in wartime, and dealing with the power of a state court to punish for contempt the publication of criticism of a trial while the trial was in progress, Justice Black in 1941 said for the Supreme Court in a five-to-four decision: "What finally emerges from the 'clear and present danger' cases is a working principle that the substantive evil must be extremely serious and the degree of imminence extremely high before utterances can be punished." [31] The majority did not find here enough danger to justify punishment. Rather, it used the Fourteenth Amendment as a basis for reading an extreme interpretation of the clear and present danger doctrine into the Constitution. Justice Frankfurter, who has been thought of by his admirers as the heir of Holmes and Brandeis, dissented against this interpretation of the Fourteenth Amendment as incorporating the prohibitions of the First, but steered his way around the clear and present danger doctrine. Dissenting in a similar case five years later, however, he contended:

> "Clear and present danger" was never used by Mr. Justice Holmes to express a technical legal doctrine or to convey a formula for adjudicating cases. It was a literary phrase not to be distorted by being taken from its context. In its setting it served to indicate the importance of freedom of speech to a free society but also to emphasize that its exercise must be compatible with the preservation of other freedoms essential to a democracy and guaranteed by our Constitution.[32]

The judicial battle over the scope of the clear and present danger doctrine continued through the period of World War II into the cold-war period that followed, and became involved in cold-war issues. The Labor Management Relations Act of 1947, better known as the Taft-Hartley Act, reflected more than a conservative reaction against the measure of government support given to organized labor by the National Labor Relations Act of 1935. It also reflected disillusionment with our recent Soviet ally and fear of the penetration of Communist influence into labor unions. It provided that as a condition of giving unions the benefits of the statute the officers of unions must take an oath denying membership in or affiliation with the Communist party and denying belief or membership in any organization that believed, taught, or advocated the forcible or otherwise illegal overthrow of the

United States government. One of the specific purposes of the provision was to prevent political strikes by unions under the direction of Communist leaders. Resisting unions contended that the statute could be upheld only on a showing that political strikes constituted a clear and present danger.

The Supreme Court treated the doctrine as still in good standing, but the decision represented a conservative drift in application. It was not, said Chief Justice Vinson for the Court, a mechanical test. Furthermore,

> in suggesting that the substantive evil must be serious and substantial, it was never the intention of this Court to lay down an absolutist test measured in terms of danger to the Nation. When the effect of a statute or ordinance upon the exercise of First Amendment freedoms is relatively small and the public interest to be protected is substantial, it is obvious that a rigid test requiring a showing of imminent danger to the security of the Nation is an absurdity.[33]

Only Justice Black dissented squarely from the decision of the Court as a whole, and he put his emphasis on the prohibitions of the First Amendment generally rather than on the clear and present danger doctrine. He found the statute an invasion not only of freedom of speech but also of belief, and as to freedom of belief, he seemed to find in the First Amendment an absolute protection against invasion of it.

The culminating case of *Dennis v. United States,* decided in 1951, left interpretation of the clear and present danger doctrine in still greater confusion. After one of the roughest courtroom battles on record against the obstructive tactics so well worked out by Communist discipline, eleven Communist party leaders had been convicted for violation of the conspiracy provisions of the Smith Act of 1940. The defendants appealed on the ground of violation of the First and Fifth Amendments. One of the few things that can be said with certainty about the decision is that six justices voted to sustain the conviction, two dissented, and one did not participate. The majority of six required three opinions to express their assent, so that there was no opinion of the Court. Each of the dissenters wrote an opinion. In other words, there were five opinions to portray the diverse positions of eight justices.

The Smith Act, in part a substitute for the Sedition Act of the period of World War I, which had been repealed after the close of that war, made it unlawful to advocate or teach the overthrow of the government by force or violence or to organize or help organize a group to that end, or to conspire to do these things. The defendants challenged enforcement of the statute against them, partly on the ground that their activity in organizing and leading the Communist party did not create a clear and present danger, and that they were therefore denied their rights under the First Amendment. Of the majority justices, Chief Justice Vinson, speaking for himself and three others, found that a clear and present danger did exist. Justice Frankfurter upheld conviction largely on other grounds. Justice Jackson found no denial of a constitutional right, whether or not a clear and present danger existed. Of the two dissenters, Justice Douglas contended that a clear and present danger had not been shown, and Justice Black talked not at all about this doctrine but about the First Amendment generally.

Because of the importance of the evolution of the doctrine in connection with the preservation of liberties—or the exercise of protective power, if the emphasis is to be put on power rather than liberty—it is well to deal more at length with the positions of some of the authors of opinions. Chief Justice Vinson repeated his attack upon constitutional absolutism, saying:

> Speech is not an absolute, above and beyond control by the legislature when its judgment, subject to review here, is that certain kinds of speech are so undesirable as to warrant criminal sanction. Nothing is more certain in modern society than the principle that there are no absolutes, that a name, a phrase, a standard has meaning only when associated with the considerations which gave birth to the nomenclature. . . . To those who would paralyze our government in the face of impending threat by encasing it in a semantic straitjacket we must reply that all concepts are relative.[34]

He found overthrow of government by force and violence a substantial enough interest to justify limitation of freedom of speech. An attempt to that end, even though doomed to failure for want of numbers or power, was an evil of such potency that Congress could act to prevent it; it constituted a clear and present danger, whether or not there was probability of success. The Chief Justice apparently fixed his mind not on an alleged clear and present danger of the overthrow of the government but on the danger involved in the conspiracy to attempt such overthrow, whether or not it was successful. In short, he and his three colleagues went a long way toward devitalizing the doctrine as originally announced. While adhering to the language of the doctrine they were back in the area of bad tendency, or manifest tendency, which in earlier years had been sponsored by justices who had refused to speak in terms of clear and present danger.

Justice Frankfurter thought that drawing the line between the power of the government to protect itself and the rights covered by the First Amendment involved competing interests that must be defined by the legislature rather than by the courts, as long as the legislative judgment reached was not outside the pale of fairness.

> Free-speech cases are not an exception to the principle that we are not legislators, that direct policy-making is not our province. How best to reconcile competing interests is the business of the legislatures, and the balance they strike is a judgment not to be displaced by ours, but to be respected unless outside the pale of fair judgment.[35]

As for clear and present danger, he thought it an ill service to Justice Holmes "to make him the victim of a tendency which he fought all his life, whereby phrases are made to do service for critical analysis by being turned into dogma." [36] He concluded:

> It were far better that the phrase be abandoned than that it be sounded once more to hide from the believers in an absolute right of speech the plain fact that the interest in speech, profoundly important as it is, is no more conclusive in judicial

> review than other attributes of democracy or than a determination of the people's representatives that a measure is necessary to assure the safety of government itself.[37]

Justice Jackson thought the clear and present danger doctrine inappropriate for dealing with offenses of the nature and scope of the Communist conspiracy. He preferred to save that doctrine for use as a "rule of reason" in the type of case for which it was devised.

> When the issue is criminality of a hot-headed speech on a street corner, or circulation of a few incendiary pamphlets, or parading by some zealots behind a red flag, or refusal of a handful of school children to salute our flag, it is not beyond the capacity of the judicial process to gather, comprehend, and weigh the necessary materials for decision whether it is a clear and present danger of substantive evil or a harmless letting off of steam. It is not a prophecy, for the danger in such cases has matured by the time of the trial or it was never present.[38]

Justice Black, by contrast, in this case taking the First Amendment almost as an absolute prohibition, refused to treat the issue as one to be settled by a judicial determination of reasonableness.

> So long as this Court exercises the power of judicial review of legislation, I cannot agree that the First Amendment permits us to sustain laws suppressing freedom of speech and press on the basis of Congress' or our own notions of mere "reasonableness." Such a doctrine waters down the First Amendment so that it amounts to little more than an admonition to Congress.[39]

Voicing again his belief in the "preferred position" of civil liberties, he concluded with the statement: "There is hope . . . that in calmer times, when present pressures, passions and fears subside, this or some later Court will restore the First Amendment liberties to the high preferred place where they belong in a free society." [40]

Finally, Justice Douglas thought that there was a time when even speech lost its constitutional immunity, and he deemed the clear and present danger doctrine the rightful measure of authority. He found no such danger here, since the Communist party as a political party in the United States was a group of little consequence without sufficient numbers to permit the winning of elections. As a political faction in the United States it had already been destroyed, not by repression but by the power of free speech. Since the defendants were politically impotent in the United States, there was no such danger as would permit governmental restraint of the freedom of those "miserable merchants of unwanted ideas." [41]

So it is, therefore, that by 1951 there was so much conflict of opinion as to the meaning and scope of the clear and present danger doctrine, and so much doubt concerning its use in various types of cases, that it had lost most of its meaning as a standard for measuring the limits of permissible conduct by government. True, it did not face competition from any other generally accepted test. About the only thing we could be sure of as a result of a long sequence of cases was that in those involving subversion the Court as then constituted would play the situation by ear, and would play it without harmony and with a tremendous amount of institutional discord.

3 Before dealing further with the Supreme Court in relation to sedition and parallel offenses, it seems best to go back to earlier periods for discussion of the status of groups that are particularly suspect when issues of subversion are raised: namely, aliens and naturalized citizens who may have a residual or dominant loyalty to some other country that is dangerous to the United States. Congress recognized the danger as early as the international crisis in 1798 in an amendment to the Naturalization Act extending from five to fourteen years the period of residence necessary for the attainment of citizenship. It was earnestly urged, indeed, that the right to citizenship should be restricted only to persons born in the United States.[42] "An Act Concerning Aliens" gave the President virtually unlimited power to deport aliens whom he thought dangerous. "An Act Respecting Enemy Aliens," containing no time limit, became a permanent basis for restriction of the activities

of enemy aliens or their deportation from the United States. After the period of World War I, when enemy aliens were made exceedingly uncomfortable in the United States, though not more so than in other countries, Congress passed an act to promote the elimination of undesirable aliens by authorizing deportation of aliens who had violated war statutes. The Supreme Court rejected the contention that deportation was punishment and subject to the restrictions by which the power to punish was hedged. Said Chief Justice Taft: "The right to expel aliens is a sovereign power, necessary to the safety of the country, and only limited by treaty obligations in respect thereto, entered into with other governments." [43]

National policy with respect to immigration, deportation, and the granting of American citizenship has been affected by the alleged unassimilability of particular groups—for example, of certain Oriental peoples; by attitudes toward aliens as competitors with American labor; and by a supposed threat to American institutions and American security, as in the instance, particularly, of Fascists, Nazis, and Communists. In general it can be said that our policy with respect to aliens has been growing more and more restrictive since the period of World War I, for reasons that of course include the congestion of population as well as the fear of subversive conduct of one kind or another. The quota basis for immigration is calculated to give a maximum allowance to countries that provided the original stock of American people and to minimize the influx of those most different from the original stock.

World War II brought new crises with respect to immigration and deportation. Since an immigrant has no constitutional right to enter the United States, and the would-be immigrant is usually in no position to assert a claim, the Supreme Court seldom has to deal with that issue. It was approached obliquely, however, in the case of Ellen Knauff, a woman of German nationality, who sought admission under the War Brides Act of 1945, a statute to facilitate the entry of wives of American servicemen who married while abroad. Without a hearing, however, and without disclosure of grounds, Ellen Knauff was stopped at Ellis Island and held for deportation on an order from the Attorney General. Habeas corpus proceedings were instituted to test the right of the Attorney General so to exclude her. When the case reached the Supreme Court, Justice Minton as its spokesman reasserted the position that an alien could claim no right to enter the United States. Entrance was a privilege to be granted on such terms as the government saw fit to prescribe. The right to exclude aliens stemmed not alone from legislative power but was inherent in the executive power to control the foreign affairs of the nation. It was not within the province of a court to review the determination of the political branch of the government to exclude a given alien.

Only seven justices participated in the decision, and three of them dissented. Justice Frankfurter, speaking for himself alone, expressed the belief that the right conveyed by the statute was not a right to the alien but to the American husband, and that it could not be denied in this arbitrary fashion. Justice Jackson, speaking for all three dissenters, said:

> Congress will have to use more explicit language than any yet cited before I will agree that it has authorized an administrative officer to break up the family of an American citizen without notice or charges, evidence of guilt and a chance to meet it.
>
> I should direct the Attorney General either to produce his evidence justifying exclusion or to admit Mrs. Knauff to the country.[44]

It is largely irrelevant to this discussion that Mrs. Knauff was finally released for entry into the United States, after some three years spent at Ellis Island, on recommendation of the Immigration and Naturalization Service. The significant fact was that, in spite of the argument of three dissenting justices, the right of an alien to enter the United States remained subject to the will or to the whim of the executive branch of the government.

During the war it was possible for the government under the still potent Alien Enemy Act of 1798 to remove alien enemies from the country with or without formal administrative proceedings—provided, of course, that it could find a place to which it could practicably deport them. When military hostilities had ended, but before peace had been proclaimed, the government repatriated to Germany some Germans who had been interned here during the war. In 1946 one of them, Kurt Ludecke, was ordered deported under the continued exercise of the war power. He contended that since the war was now over he could not be so removed, and that he had been denied the fair hearing that due process required. The Supreme Court held that the President, as authorized by Congress, was the appropriate agency to determine when war ended and that the question was not subject to judicial review. But here again the Court was divided, by a vote of five to four. The four thought it a pure fiction that we were still at war with Germany in terms of the statute. Justice Black suggested, in the light of the refusal to inquire into the fairness of the hearing, that "because of today's opinion individual liberty will be less secure tomorrow than it was yesterday." [45] Three of the four justices contended that even if Ludecke was still an alien enemy, he was entitled to due notice and a fair hearing.

> The notion that the discretion of any officer of government can override due process is foreign to our system. Due process does not perish when war comes. It is well established that the war power does not remove constitutional limitations safeguarding essential liberties.[46]

The contention was significant in terms of the rights of aliens and also in terms of war issues, which will be discussed in the following chapter.

As for cases dealing with deportation of aliens already lawfully in the United States, most of the important ones have had to do with people deemed dangerous to the United States because of Communist affiliations. Unfortunately the issues until recent years were obscured by the fact that the persons to be deported were by some conservative and influential people deemed dangerous and subject to deportations not so much because of Communist affiliations, which provided the legal basis of action, as because of liberal ideas generally and sponsorship of the cause of organized labor. The issues were thus obscured in the case of Harry Bridges, a highly controversial labor leader from Australia, whose offense in the eyes of his enemies was not merely that he was alleged to be promoting Communism among longshoremen in the Pacific area but that he promoted effective union action in a region where the organization of labor as such was still being fought. Time after time, efforts were made to have Bridges deported to his native land. This strategy is revealed in part in a concurring opinion written by Justice Murphy in 1945:

> Seldom if ever in the history of this nation has there been such a concentrated and relentless crusade to deport an individual because he dared to exercise the freedom that belongs to him as a human being and that is guaranteed to him by the Constitution.[47]

The struggle to bring about deportation continued even after Bridges had become an American citizen, through efforts to have his certificate of naturalization canceled so that he might be treated as an undesirable alien. The purpose here is not to pass upon the question whether Bridges was or was not a Communist who ought to have been deported; it is merely to stress the fact that for a number of years the motives of the advocates of deportation were so intermixed that people deeply loyal to the United States doubted the good faith of the proceedings because of the interjection of irrelevant economic issues. The confusion carried over into many other cases.

Deportation proceedings for Communist affiliation, however—or for membership in any group advocating the overthrow of the government by force and violence—were carried on against many persons who were not known to be objectionable for any reasons other than Communist connections. The Supreme Court had held in 1939 that the statute then in force applied only to current membership and not to past membership that had been terminated.[48] To protect its alien members the Communist party then dropped them from its rolls. Recognizing the move for the subterfuge it was, Congress enacted the Alien Registration Act of 1940 which, in addition to requiring the registration of aliens and the keeping of a continuing record of their location, authorized deportation for past membership even though such membership had been terminated. In *Harisiades v. Shaughnessy*,[49] decided in 1952, the Supreme Court upheld the deportation of a man from Greece, a man from Italy, and a woman from Russia, all of whom had been party members at some time in the past but had long since ceased to be members. The defendants claimed that they were being denied the right to due process, freedom of speech, and immunity against ex post facto laws that prevented punishment for acts not criminal at the time they were committed. The Supreme Court, however, adhered to the position that the right to deport aliens was absolute and that deportation was a civil rather than a criminal action, so that the defendants were not being "punished" in the legal sense, however drastic the deprivation of privileges might be. Only Justices Douglas and Black contended that deportation was punishment and that the aliens, being lawfully in this country, were entitled to the protections the Constitution conferred upon "persons." Said Justice Douglas:

> [Congress] has ordered these aliens deported not for what they are but for what they once were. Perhaps a hearing would show that they continue to be people dangerous and hostile to us. But the principle of forgiveness and the doctrine of redemption are too deep in our philosophy to admit that there is no return for those who have once erred.[50]

In 1954, in *Galvan v. Press*, the Supreme Court adhered to its position in enforcing the even more drastic Internal Security Act of 1950, upholding deportation of a Mexican who with his family had been in the United States for a third of a century and who had been a member of the Communist party from 1944 to 1946. In the opinion of the Court Justice Frankfurter remarked:

In the light of the expansion of the concept of substantive due process as a limitation upon all powers of Congress, even the war power . . . , much could be said for the view, were we writing on a clean slate, that the due process clause qualifies the scope of political discretion heretofore recognized as belonging to Congress in regulating the entry and deportation of aliens. And since the intrinsic consequences of deportation are so close to punishment for crime, it might fairly be said also that the ex post facto clause, even though applicable only to punitive legislation, should be applied to deportation.

But the slate is not clean. . . . And whatever might have been said at an earlier date for applying the ex post facto clause, it has been the unbroken rule of this Court that it has no application to deportation.[51]

Justices Black and Douglas dissented in spite of the fact that the slate was not clean. Said the latter:

This action is hostile to our constitutional standards. . . . Aliens who live here in peace, who do not abuse our hospitality, who are law-abiding members of our communities, have the right to due process of law. They too are "persons" within the meaning of the Fifth Amendment. They can be molested by the government in times of peace only when their presence here is hostile to the safety or welfare of the Nation. If they are to be deported, it must be for what they are and do, not for what they once believed.[52]

It is true that according to past decisions aliens in this country are entitled to the constitutional protections accorded to "persons" with respect to the ordinary problems of living here.[53] But it remains to be seen whether the dissenting minority can so influence the majority as to secure these rights with respect to deportation. It may well be that the Court will continue to recognize the absolute power the political branches of the government claim to possess, although the erosion of that doctrine is by no means beyond the range of possibility.

4 Although aliens could be summarily deported as the government saw fit, naturalized citizens with a sense of loyalty to foreign countries hostile to the United States could not.

The latter could be deported only if they could be deprived of their citizenship. Periods of strain have shown American citizens reflecting deep fealty to the lands of their origin, whether Germany, Italy, the Soviet Union, or some other country. It was widely believed, indeed, that many aliens had acquired American citizenship for the deliberate purpose of ensuring their constitutional right to remain in the United States and work for its enemies. Citizenship papers could be canceled, and the possessors returned to the status of aliens subject to deportation, if fraud in the naturalization process could be proved, but proof was often difficult. During World War II the Department of Justice attempted widespread denaturalization of citizens showing partisanship on behalf of the lands of their birth but found themselves stopped by the Supreme Court, which refused to accept current behavior alone as proof of bad faith in taking the oath of loyalty to the United States at some earlier time. From a concurring opinion by Justice Rutledge in one of the cases, it is apparent that the Court was concerned not so much about the welfare of particular litigants as about millions of naturalized citizens who would have to hedge their conduct more carefully than natural-born citizens in order to avoid possible challenge to their status as citizens—they would be left, in effect, as second-class citizens.

> No citizen with such a threat hanging over his head could be free. If he belonged to "off-color" organizations or held too radical or, perhaps, too reactionary views, for some segment of the judicial palate, when his admission took place, he could not open his mouth without fear his words would be held against him.[54]

The rather considerable program of denaturalization therefore had to be abandoned.

More serious during World War II was the curbing of rights of American-born citizens who, because of their race and color, were deemed suspect on the ground of possible superior loyalty to Japan, under the laws of which they had or could have dual citizenship. Here, as in the instance of some aliens, illustrated above, there was a mixture of motives. Groups of people on the West Coast had long resented business competition from thrifty Americans of Japanese ancestry in their midst and their possession of valuable property. Fear that war enemies might be hidden among the loyal yellow people accentuated the desire to curb their activities and to get them out of that region, permanently if possible. On the basis of a presidential proclamation and an act of Congress in support of military orders, military authorities on the West Coast, at a time when invasion was feared, established a curfew law for all persons of Japanese ancestry, requiring them to be in their place of residence from 8:00 P.M. to 6:00 A.M. The Supreme Court unanimously upheld the order, noting that "the danger of espionage and sabotage, in time of war and of threatened invasion, calls upon the military authorities to scrutinize every relevant fact bearing on the loyalty of populations in the danger areas." [55]

With Justices Roberts and Murphy dissenting, the Court also upheld the exclusion of American citizens of Japanese ancestry from certain areas altogether, areas where other civilian citizens were permitted to remain.[56] The majority of the Court avoided discussion of the constitutionality of the most drastic of the measures taken, that incarcerating thousands of Japanese-Americans in relocation centers, where, however humane the treatment offered, the persons involved were held prisoners without any conviction or even accusation of any crime. In the relevant case the Court held that neither the statute nor the executive orders based on it justified the detention. It seemed to imply that the program would have been unconstitutional had it been authorized. Justices Roberts and Murphy insisted on making this point in concurring opinions.[57] Viewing the question retrospectively, it is probable that the Court regarded the entire program with respect to Japanese-Americans as a most unfortunate affair.[58]

5 From this discussion of groups that, because of national origin or racial composition, were believed to require special

watching on the basis of danger of subversion, we turn to those who have special opportunities for subversion because of their employment or for other reasons. Particularly important in this category are people working for the federal government who have special opportunity for spying and obstruction and who may exercise those opportunities if their loyalties are to foreign powers or to ideologies that logically dictate alien loyalties.

Apart from subversive activities during our occasional wars, we have had in the United States little experience with basic disloyalty, or at any rate with disloyalty that was clearly dangerous. The result has been that in recent years, with the ugly problem of Communist subversion to the fore, we have had to operate with little background of sound experience. We have probably been at once so severe and arbitrary as to curb unjustly many rights possessed under the Constitution and so lax or inefficient in our methods as to leave ourselves dangerously exposed. The cold-war period has been one of experimentation with techniques of self-protection, by methods often at once drastic and ineffective. Yet it has been necessary to learn, and experimentation has been the only means of learning. Familiar, at least in a general way, is the story of the establishment and operation of loyalty boards in the several major administrative agencies of the government to check on personnel that might be dangerous, and of a central Loyalty Review Board. Familiar also, and slightly humorous were it not so serious, is the story of the Attorney General who, like Ko-Ko in Gilbert and Sullivan's *The Mikado,* had his list of organizations whose members "never would be missed" if separated from government service. Familiar also, although now rapidly slipping from memory, is the story of the confusion in 1953, and for a time thereafter, of loyalty to the United States with loyalty to a political regime, and the war of nerves that was waged among personnel who were in office at the time of a change in administration. Out of the confused efforts to do a difficult job that had to be done came a few important cases dealing with critical aspects of the problem, and a great diversity of Supreme Court opinion leading off in many directions.

Important among the cases to reach the Supreme Court was *Joint Anti-Fascist Refugee Committee v. McGrath,*[59] decided in 1951, which had to do with the use of the Attorney General's list. The list, carrying the names of organizations that the Attorney General by undisclosed methods, without notice and hearing, had found to be subversive, was circulated to the several agencies of the government to bring about dismissal of government workers who might be members. The organizations listed, even if perchance they were subversive, saw to it that they had ostensible purposes that were quite legitimate. The Joint Anti-Fascist Refugee Committee, for example, one of the three organizations involved in the case, had collected from donors and disbursed to anti-Fascist refugees well over a million dollars. Publication of its name on the Attorney General's list could be expected to stop or drastically check the flow of contributions, particularly from government workers who, because of connection with the organization, could expect to be deprived of their employment. The suit was to compel the removal of the names of certain organizations from the list. The lower courts dismissed the complaints because of want of a cause of action or want of standing to sue.

By a vote of five to three the Supreme Court reversed the lower court decisions, with the result that the complaints were ordered to be reinstated. Yet so diverse were the positions of the majority that the five justices required space for five opinions to say what they had to say. The three dissenting justices joined in one long opinion. Because of their diversity the six majority and minority opinions completely defy summary here. It can only be said that they reflected the confusion of the entire country as it adjusted to the unprecedented experience of coping with potential disloyalty that went to the core of our society and showed its ugly head among people who in this land of idealization of equality were thought of as the "best people." The five majority justices were shocked at the defamation of private organizations by government action without resort to prescribed methods with prescribed protections; yet the eight participating justices were in varying degrees aware that methods had to be devised for coping with the menace of disloyalty and that the methods might force changes in hitherto required procedures.

Pursuant to the decision the Refugee Committee case was returned to the United States district court of its origin for reinstatement of the complaint. The district judge there found that only four of the Supreme Court justices, and hence not a majority of the Court, had held that notice and hearing were necessary before the Attorney General could place an organization on the proscribed list. Hence notice and hearing were not now to be required. In the meantime, furthermore, while still refusing to disclose the sources of information used by the F.B.I., the Attorney General provided the district court with a summary of the information on which he—or his predecessor—had acted. The information was that, although the Refugee Committee did indeed disburse funds to anti-Fascist refugees from the Spanish civil war, it had been organized by order of the Communist party, which supervised its actions and to which reports were made; the party had made contributions to the work of the committee; party publications had supported the work of the committee; the committee aided in the subversive work of the party, and brought to this country as refugees agents to assist in supervising the subversive work of the party.[60] The district court denied the complaint.

The district court having acted on the merits of the complaint, the Supreme Court refused to review its action.[61] Although the grounds for refusal to review the decision were not explained, it may be assumed that the Supreme Court still lacked a majority willing to hold that an organization was entitled to notice and hearing before being placed on the Attorney General's list.

Another attack on the government's loyalty program was

made by an employee who was removed from office on grounds of disloyalty. Dorothy Bailey, an employee of the Federal Security Agency, in a nonsensitive position, was removed after hearings before the regional board and the Loyalty Review Board. She challenged the legality and the constitutionality of her removal on the ground, among others, that she had been denied an opportunity to face witnesses against her, the benefits of a judicial trial, and her rights under the First Amendment. With one judge dissenting, the United States Court of Appeals for the District of Columbia denied her claim. The court held that a government employee could be dismissed for any reason or for no reason and that there had been no denial of constitutional right.[62] The Supreme Court, equally divided, affirmed the judgment,[63] and, as is customary when the Court is equally divided, presented no opinions. In the Refugee case, however, Justice Douglas illuminated the issues by criticism of the Bailey case, calling it "an excellent illustration of how dangerous a departure from our constitutional standards can be." [64] Concerning the informers against Dorothy Bailey, the chairman of the Loyalty Review Board had said, "I haven't the slightest knowledge as to who they were or how active they have been in anything." [65]

Denouncing what was in effect a trial for disloyalty on the basis of unsifted evidence from unknown persons, Justice Douglas contended that while technically Dorothy Bailey was not subjected to a trial on a criminal charge,

> she was on trial for her reputation, her job, her professional standing. A disloyalty trial is the most crucial event in the life of a public servant. If condemned, he is branded for life as a person unworthy of trust or confidence. To make that condemnation without meticulous regard for the decencies of a fair trial is abhorrent to fundamental justice.[66]

Noting that every government employee was required to take an oath of loyalty, he contended that the proper procedure in cases of this kind was prosecution for perjury, where all the safeguards of the Bill of Rights were afforded. Justices who took the opposite position, however, refrained from stating their views.

In 1955 a further attempt was made to get a Supreme Court appraisal of the process of removing government employees on the basis of accusations of disloyalty by "faceless informers," who were often unknown even to the boards acting on the charges. The challenge was offered by John P. Peters, a doctor of medicine at Yale University, who for a per diem fee was often called to Washington to give professional advice to the Public Health Service. By his agency board Dr. Peters was cleared of charges made against him by some unknown source. The Loyalty Review Board, however, on its own motion re-examined the case and ordered dismissal on grounds of disloyalty. Dr. Peters apparently had little interest in the employment but resented the attack on his reputation. He appealed to the Supreme Court after the administrative action had been approved on the basis of the Bailey case.

The Supreme Court again avoided the constitutional question, this time not on the basis of equal division but on the ground that the Loyalty Review Board had had no power to intervene in the case. Said Chief Justice Warren for the Court:

> In this Court, petitioner urges us to decide the case on the constitutional issues. These issues, if reached by the Court, would obviously present serious and far-reaching problems in reconciling fundamental constitutional guarantees with the procedures used to determine the loyalty of government personnel. . . . We find, however, that the case can be decided without reaching the constitutional issues.[67]

Only Justices Black and Douglas discussed the constitutional questions. Said the latter:

> We have here a system where government with all its power and authority condemns a man to a suspect class and the outer darkness, without the rudiments of a fair trial. The practice of using faceless informers has apparently spread through a vast

domain. It is used not only to get rid of employees in the government, but also employees who work for private firms having contracts with the government. It has touched countless hundreds of men and women and ruined many. It is an un-American practice which we should condemn.[68]

6 The scope of the rights of federal employees is not much illuminated by Supreme Court decisions with respect to restrictive laws of the states. Although subversion of American institutions can take place in connection with state as well as federal government, the state governments are at least one step away from responsibility for loyalty on the frontiers of international relations. With Justices Black and Douglas dissenting, the Court upheld the requirement of a loyalty oath of city employees,[69] and New York's Feinberg law authorizing public school authorities to dismiss employees who, after notice and hearing, were found to advocate the overthrow of government by unlawful means or were unable to explain membership in subversive organizations.[70] Yet the entire Court, with a multiplicity of opinions, struck down an Oklahoma statute that barred from teaching positions persons who had at some time been connected with proscribed organizations, whether or not they knew of the subversive character of the organizations.[71] In 1956, by a vote of five to four, it struck down, too, a New York statute that denied teaching privileges to any person who had refused to testify in any proceeding on the ground that his testimony might incriminate him.[72]

In connection with the latter case, not too much should be taken for granted regarding restriction on the power of a state to curb employment. The Court was here deeply concerned about the derisive attacks being made on what irresponsible politicians called "Fifth Amendment Communists," and about the assumption that claiming the right to avoid self-incrimination given by the Fifth Amendment was a tacit admission of guilt. Although the defendant here involved was a state employee, his refusal to testify and his claim of the

Fifth Amendment privilege had been made in connection with the work of a United States Senate investigating committee. The right to claim immunity, said Justice Clark for the Court, was one of the most valuable prerogatives of the citizen. It would be reduced to a hollow mockery if its exercise could be taken as a confession of guilt or a conclusive presumption of perjury.[73]

The Supreme Court has tried indirectly to keep control of subversive activities in the federal government rather than permit duplicating and perhaps conflicting control by the states. Striking down a state sedition act on the ground that Congress had already occupied the field, so that the states were excluded from it, the Court noted in 1956 that forty-two states and two territories had had sedition acts under varying titles. Pointing to danger of interference with the federal program, Chief Justice Warren approvingly quoted the court below as saying: "Sedition against the United States is *not* a local offense. It is a crime against the *Nation.* As such, it should be prosecuted and punished in the federal courts where this defendant has in fact been prosecuted and convicted and is now under sentence." [74] Although some zealous members of Congress disliked the decision and sought to amend the federal statute to permit the states to share the field, there is likelihood that the policy announced by the Court will be permitted to stand.

As to action by the federal government, whereas only a minority of the justices committed themselves to opposition to the use of "faceless witnesses" to get government employees dismissed for disloyalty, a majority checked the process of convicting in court by use of professional witnesses who were employed by the government and moved from case to case, and who were eventually caught in the delivery of false testimony.[75] Yet it is obvious that a great deal of time will be required to refine procedures for dealing with the evils of subversion in such a way as to eliminate the evils seemingly inherent in the procedures themselves.

7 In summary, it can be said that if the Supreme Court has had difficulty in giving shape to the law of the Constitution where subversion is involved, the difficulties have lain primarily in the complexities of the task itself and have been only incidentally the product of the character or the personnel of the Court. With respect to treason, the Court has been hobbled by restrictions of constitutional definition and procedure, and it has probably felt, through courts of original jurisdiction, both an excessive eagerness to convict in highly emotionalized cases and a corresponding unwillingness to convict because of the stigma attached to this particular crime.

But the greater difficulty has derived from the lack of clear demarcation between loyalty and patriotism on the one hand and disloyalty and subversion on the other. As well discussed by Morton Grodzins in a recent book,[76] people tend to possess not a single loyalty, as to their own nation, but a complex of loyalties to nation, family, racial group, local community, profession, religion, political group, and other units. These loyalties inevitably give rise to conflict within the person himself and within a given society. A great deal of sympathy with Communism in the 1930's and thereafter marked not basic disloyalty to the United States, as was later assumed by professional red-baiters: it marked rather a deep disillusionment with control in the United States by an element that permitted, and presumably could not have prevented within the pattern of its own ideology, the great depression that devastated the country before the advent of the New Deal. Large numbers of indignant and restless young people were convinced that the Communist way was the new American way. In their own minds they were not subversives but true American patriots. It took time and ugly experience with the Communist party to demonstrate that Communism in the United States was primarily the working of a ruthless and malevolent foreign power. By contrast, the Old Guard in American thinking saw subversion not merely in Communism but also in the New Deal and indeed in any form of ameliorative legislation, feeling that the depression had been inevitable in the course of things, that it was in some way an expression of the will of God, or the inevitable product of natural law, and ought to have been permitted to hit bottom without governmental interference, in spite of any additional suffering that might result. These conservative patriots were to liberal thinkers the real subversives, the real traitors to American welfare.

Behind the inability of the Supreme Court to arrive at unanimous decisions with respect to loyalty and subversion has lain an understanding that the pattern of patriotism changes with changing conceptions of welfare and that, as the present is hard to appraise, so the future is hard to predict. Although it is not completely true that today's traitor may well be tomorrow's patriot and vice versa, there is enough volatility in the concept of patriotism that such a statement might well be made respecting many of the offenders who are brought to the bar of American courts. Thoughtful judges are well aware of the ironic significance of Morton Grodzins' comment on British experience with William Joyce, the "Lord Haw-Haw" of World War II infamy. After the war Joyce was hanged for treason for offenses that included broadcasting programs intended to interfere with conduct of the war between England and Germany. At the time of his trial, any other result would have been unthinkable. Yet from the vantage point of later years we can see that one of his purposes was to bring about united action between Great Britain and Germany against the Soviet Union. Such advocacy today would seem anything but treasonable. The former enemy has slipped into the category of an acceptable ally, and the former ally has become at least a cold-war enemy. Lord Haw-Haw, if living today, might well be regarded as something of a patriot.[77] With such instability in our conceptions of loyalty and subversion it is only natural that courts should be hesitant and should be in conflict in working out the pattern of law.

The area of doubt, indeed, is even wider than that here

suggested. Since World War I we have been made to wonder whether loyalty to one's own nation exclusively, by contrast with a broader pattern of feeling taking in alien peoples, is quite as high an ideal as was long assumed. The course of current turbulent events, it is true, has pushed into the background such thinking as went into Wendell Willkie's *One World*, published in 1943, and the unifying goals of the League of Nations and the United Nations. As a people we would perhaps be more shocked today than we were in the 1920's by a statement such as that of Rosika Schwimmer: "I am an uncompromising pacifist. . . . I have no sense of nationalism, only a cosmic consciousness of belonging to the human family." [78] Yet for all our hatred of the methods and ideologies of Fascists, Nazis, and Communists, we may have to face, among our people and in our courts, the question whether the only American patriotism that will enable us to survive may be not patriotism to this nation alone but a sense of responsibility for and loyalty to all the peoples of the world. The Supreme Court is undoubtedly aware of the grinding pressures that would be necessary to compel us to make such a transition in our conceptions of loyalty, and of the possibility that we may become more nationalist rather than less nationalist before we shall become finally internationalist. Certain it is, in the face of the hostilities raging throughout the world, that the expansion of our loyalties to take in all mankind will be a slow and difficult process. In the midst of the turmoil we cannot expect too much clarity from the Supreme Court in the statement and application of principles of law with respect to the threat of subversion.

IV *The Place of the Military*

Interrelated as the issues involving the place of the military in our governmental system are with the threat of subversion, discussed in the preceding chapter, the topic has unique features of its own that require separate discussion. It is a commonplace fact of our tradition that we have had no military elite. There has been no aggregation of first families, such as existed in many European countries, from which at least one son went into the military to achieve a position of leadership [1]—somewhat as in the United States decades ago large families often designated one son for the Christian ministry. Military service has not been regarded among any large segment of our population as a high calling. As a new nation, indeed, we had learned from experience with British regulars and the hired Hessian troops used against us to distrust and dislike professional soldiers as a class. Recognizing the necessity of community defense, we voiced the ideal of the citizen soldier, of the farmer who left his plow in the field to head for the battlefield, of the frontiersman who kept his rifle standing against a tree close by or stood it in the corner of the community church for convenient use against marauding Indians. We assumed that every American knew or could quickly learn how to shoot and that courage and marksmanship were the prime requisites of the good soldier.

Furthermore, with a distrust for standing armies even when they might be necessary, the framers of the Constitution used the federal structure and the separation of powers to divide authority and prevent its concentration for tyrannical purposes. They left with the states the power to maintain a militia, which in time of national crisis might be called into national service but which would inevitably retain a considerable amount of state coloration. They gave Congress the power to raise and support armies and to provide and maintain a navy and to declare war, but they designated the President as the commander in chief of the army and navy. The early congresses carried out the intent of the framers by setting up war and navy departments with civilian heads to manage army and navy affairs, with appointive power in the President, subject to the consent of the Senate, and control of expenditures in Congress, where by tradition bills providing for expenditures, like bills for raising revenue, have had to originate in the House of Representatives. In short, military power was so divided as to reduce to a minimum the possibility that any official or any group could use it for dictatorial purposes.

It is a familiar story that reliance on state militia, officered and trained, if trained at all, under state jurisdiction, proved tragically inadequate during the War of 1812, however necessary it may have been to reduce the danger of putting military control in the hands of a dangerous man or group. Ineptness revealed itself in later wars in spite of federal appropriations for the National Guard—the new name for the militia—and in spite of a considerable amount of federal training. For all the service rendered by the National Guard, it became apparent by the time of World War I that the federal government had to have not merely a nucleus of a fighting force of its own but a powerful striking force of men selected and trained and officered under centralized supervision. The problem of division of control between the federal government and the states has not been completely resolved, but it is no longer a major defect in our military setup. The division of military authority between the federal government and the states has thus lost most of its importance. The division of power between Congress and the President has remained important, with the President usually the victor in time of war and with Congress reasserting or having restored to it a measure of its prerogative when war is not on the immediate horizon. The competition for power between these two branches of government has a bearing on what is our main concern here—the Supreme Court's view of the relation of the military to civil government and to civilians generally.[2]

1 Because of the competition between the legislative and executive branches for power over the military and over related problems of supply, it is well to begin with a brief statement concerning the impact of constitutional war powers beyond the military field, rather than with the immediate problem of civil-military conflict and rivalry. The President is of course President as well as commander in chief of the army and navy. The Constitution clearly defines neither his power as President nor his power as commander in chief. The scope of power in both fields has had to be worked out over many years of constitutional interpretation, through a step-by-step process and without arrival at the definition the Constitution failed to provide. Furthermore, such delineations of power as may seem to be implied in the Constitution tend to be obscured by the fact that Congress can play its part

with respect to the military only by conferring power on the President or some subordinate agency of the executive branch, so that it is often hard to tell whether the President is acting by virtue of his inherent authority as President, or as commander in chief, or as the agent of Congress who by the Constitution is commanded to take care that the laws shall be faithfully executed. It has often happened, indeed, that a President eager to act without threat of restraint has lumped together the several sources of his power in order deliberately to obscure the question of his primary reliance. The following, Executive Order 9381, issued September 25, 1943, is almost a random sample:

> By virtue of the authority vested in me by the Constitution and the statutes, and particularly by the act of October 2, 1942, amending the Emergency Price Control Act of 1942 (56 Stat. 765), as amended by the Public Debt Act of 1943 (Public Law 34–78th Congress), as President of the United States and Commander in Chief of the Army and Navy, it is ordered that Executive Order No. 9250 of October 3, 1942, entitled "Providing for the Stabilizing of the National Economy," be, and it is hereby, amended as follows. . . .[3]

Such an order, with recourse to one source of power if another looks inadequate, and to the aggregate of many sources if no one of the single sources seems adequate in and of itself, creates a maximum of confusion for those who seek to trace the lines of power and invites abandonment of the attempt in hopeless confusion. Such executive strategy is likely to be most effective in time of major economic disturbance—Franklin D. Roosevelt learned to use it during the depression—or of major war, when the people and all officers of government are far more concerned with the immediate and effective exercise of power than with issues of legality. In the long run, however, such obfuscation is likely to bring discredit upon what has been assumed to be responsible government and to invite further deliberate confusion of matters that in the interest of good government ought to be kept clear.

Certain it is that during World War II, in justifying steps

taken for promotion of war production, the allocation of materials, the stabilization of prices, the protection against subversion, and in other fields, the executive branch of the government ranged far into the areas of group and individual freedom. In varying degrees these activities had support from Congress, but vast confusion reigned as to the jurisdiction that originated with Congress and that which belonged to the President in his capacity as civilian President or as military commander in chief. The most blatant claim to executive power was made in connection with President Roosevelt's demand for legislation to prevent wartime inflation by limiting the price of farm products. He made his initial request for legislation in April, 1942. When more than four months later Congress had failed to act he demanded action, set a deadline, and threatened to take action without the statute if Congress failed to enact it.

> I ask the Congress to take this action by the first of October. Inaction on your part by that date will leave me with an inescapable responsibility to the people of this country to see to it that the war effort is no longer imperiled by threat of economic chaos.
>
> In the event that the Congress should fail to act, and act adequately, I shall accept the responsibility, and I will act. . . .
>
> The President has the powers, under the Constitution and under congressional acts, to take measures necessary to avert a disaster which would interfere with the winning of the war. . . .
>
> There may be those who will say that, if the situation is as grave as I have stated it to be, I should use my power and act now. I can only say that I have approached this problem from every angle, and that I have decided that the course of conduct which I am following in this case is consistent with my sense of responsibility as President in time of war, and with my deep and unalterable devotion to the processes of democracy.
>
> The responsibilities of the President in wartime to protect the Nation are very grave. This total war, with our fighting fronts all over the world, makes the use of Executive power far more essential than in any previous war. . . .

After further elaboration President Roosevelt concluded with these significant paragraphs:

> I cannot tell what powers may have to be exercised in order to win this war.
>
> The American people can be sure that I will use my powers with a full sense of my responsibility to the Constitution and to my country. The American people can also be sure that I shall not hesitate to use every power vested in me to accomplish the defeat of our enemies in any part of the world where our own safety demands such defeat.
>
> When the war is won, the powers under which I act automatically revert to the people—to whom they belong.[4]

It is not here primarily important that Congress, raging at this application of the presidential lash, enacted the proposed statute. What is important for our purposes is the philosophy of executive power, expanded for war purposes not merely at the expense of the liberties of the people but also at the expense of a co-ordinate branch of the government. The language used suggests that the President, or the author of the initial draft of the message, may have been intrigued by the following statement in a speech by Winston Churchill in Parliament in 1940:

> Immense surrenders of their hard-won liberties have been voluntarily made by the British people in order to serve in time of war the cause of freedom and fair play, to which, keeping nothing back, they have devoted all that they have and all that they are. Parliament stands custodian of these surrendered liberties, and its most sacred duty will be to restore them in their fulness when victory has crowned our exertions and our perseverance.[5]

The two situations, however, were very different. Churchill portrayed the custodianship of surrendered liberties not in an independent executive acting as a rival of an independent legislature, but in Parliament, where legislative and executive powers were merged. He proclaimed "the depth and sincerity of our resolve to keep vital and active, even in the midst of our struggle for life, even under the fire of the enemy, those parliamentary institutions which have served us so well."[6] President Roosevelt, on the other hand, demanded congressional submission to his will and threatened to act without support from Congress if Congress refused to give that support. He saw the surrender of popular liberties not to the government as a whole but to himself as President.

In general throughout the war, Congress, though deeply resentful at the assumption of presidential authority, gave support not only through appropriations but also through broad grants of power to the executive branch, with very little in the way of restrictive provisions as to the exercise of the power granted. The Supreme Court upheld such measures as came before it, finding neither undue delegation nor other violation of the Constitution.[7] Qualms as to constitutionality were not to be permitted to stand in the way of concerted action to win the war.

2 In large part, although not completely, the Supreme Court also accepted military encroachments on civil jurisdiction as allegedly authorized by the President or Congress or the two together. It is with this subject, the relation of men in uniform and under military discipline to people claiming civilian status and civilian rights and protections, that we shall be concerned from this point onward, together with the extent of civil protections to which military personnel are themselves entitled under the Constitution.

Prior to the period of World War II, the subject of military encroachment on the area of civil jurisdiction was most fully discussed in the famous Milligan case, which was decided in 1866, shortly after the close of the Civil War. Then, as during the most recent of our wars, stormy emotions had for a time obliterated the calm necessary to balanced consideration of basic problems of constitutionality. In the words of Justice Davis:

> During the late wicked Rebellion the temper of the times did not allow that calmness in deliberation and discussion so necessary to correct conclusion of a purely judicial question. Then, considerations of safety were mingled with the exercise of power, and feelings and interests prevailed which are happily terminated.[8]

In that case, it will be remembered by those familiar with our constitutional history, Milligan, a citizen and resident of Indiana, had been working for the cause of the Confederacy by spreading propaganda for that cause in his own state. Although no battles were fought in Indiana and no Confederate troops were stationed on Indiana soil, the state was included in a military district for the purpose of effective organization of Union armies. Milligan, who had no connection with the military, might have been charged with treason or conspiracy to violate the laws of the United States and brought to trial in a civil court, such courts being in operation and in no direct way interrupted by the existence of the war. Instead he was arrested by the military and brought to trial by a military commission, under a presidential proclamation of 1862 that, without the support of any statute, prescribed such trials for "all rebels and insurgents, their aiders and abettors within the United States, and all persons discouraging volunteer enlistments, resisting militia drafts, or guilty of any disloyal practice, affording aid and comfort to rebels against the authority of the United States." [9] Under sentence of death, Milligan petitioned for a writ of habeas corpus, and the basic constitutional questions were taken to the Supreme Court.

The Supreme Court held that under the circumstances of the Milligan case the military had no power to try and punish a civilian. The judicial power with respect to civilians belonged to the civil courts, where all the procedural protections of the Bill of Rights were available, by contrast with the summary procedures of the military. This, said Justice Davis for the Court, was not a case of proclamation of martial law for a community in which war was being waged and where the civil authorities were overthrown. "Martial law cannot arise from a threatened invasion. The necessity must be actual and present; the invasion real, such as effectually closes the courts and deposes the civil administration." [10] And again, "Martial rule can never exist where the courts are open, and in the proper and unobstructed exercise of their jurisdiction. It is also confined to the locality of actual war." [11]

The impact of the decision, it is true, was somewhat blurred by the fact that four justices, while agreeing as to the disposition of the case, took the position that Congress, in the exercise of its war powers, might have authorized resort to military "tribunals for trial of crimes and offenses against the discipline or security of the army or against the public safety." [12] But history has given stress to the majority opinion rather than to the concurring position, and the Milligan case stands as a bulwark in defense of American liberties.

Amid the anxieties of wartime, judges, like other people, feel the pressures of patriotic sentiment. During World War I, at the argument of the Selective Draft Law Cases, Chief Justice White reprimanded a lawyer who asserted before the Court that the Conscription Act required men to participate in a war that had never received the approval of the people. "I don't think your statement has anything to do with the legal arguments," he declared sharply, "and it should not have been said to this Court. It is a very unpatriotic statement to make." [13] During the early weeks of World War II Chief Justice Stone was concerned about the inability of the administration to stir genuine war fervor and about the confusion and bungling in Washington.[14] Yet he was also concerned about the way in which the President had been reaching out for executive power in the foreign field and about decisions of the Supreme Court confirming the exercise of such power.[15] The case of *Ex parte Quirin,* decided hastily at a special session of the Court in midsummer, 1942, touched both his patriotic sentiments and his dislike of presidential authoritarianism.

The case was that of the eight saboteurs who landed on American shores, in uniform, from German submarines, four in New York and four in Florida, discarded their uniforms when they were not captured on landing, and in civilian clothes set out with the intent and equipment to engage in sabotage of American war industries. The landing was detected, however, and they were pursued and captured by the Federal Bureau of Investigation. At this time the government, the military services, and the people were still horrified at the gross negligence that had made possible the destruction of most of our Pacific fleet at Pearl Harbor a few months earlier. As if to prove both to the people and to our enemies that the United States was now on the alert and that any attack would bring quick retaliation, President Roosevelt now snapped into action with two important orders.

The first was a proclamation that he drafted as "President of the United States of America and Commander in Chief of the Army and Navy of the United States, by virtue of the authority vested in me by the Constitution and the statutes of the United States. . . ." It provided that enemies entering the United States for sabotage or other war purposes should be subject to the law of war and to the jurisdiction of military tribunals. It further provided that "such persons shall not be privileged to seek any remedy or maintain any proceeding directly or indirectly, or have any such remedy or proceeding sought in their behalf, in the courts of the United States, or of its States, territories and possessions. . . ." [16]

The second order, drafted "By virtue of the authority vested in me as President and as Commander in Chief of the Army and Navy, under the Constitution and statutes of the United States, and more particularly the Thirty-Eighth Article of War . . . ," set up a military tribunal of seven officers for the trial of the saboteurs. The order required that the concurrence of at least two thirds of the members should be necessary for conviction and that "The record of the trial, including any judgment or sentence, shall be transmitted directly to me for my action thereon." [17]

The military commission proceeded at once to the trial of the saboteurs, operating in strict secrecy. As a military tribunal it operated, of course, without the body of protections guaranteed by the Constitution for civil trials, although it is to be noted that the treatment afforded the defendants was by no means the harsh and summary treatment they would have gotten under similar circumstances in the country from which they came. Among the protections afforded by the commission was the aid of defense counsel appointed by the commission, in the persons of military officers who were also lawyers. In the brief time allotted to them, these lawyers gave all the zeal to the case that they would have given to clients of their own selection in the civil courts. They quickly reached the conclusion that, particularly in the light of the Milligan case, the President had exceeded his powers in closing the civil courts to the defendants and in ordering trial by military commission. They further contended that the commission had not been set up according to existing provisions of the Articles of War, and they were disturbed about the review of the decision, which was to be only in the President himself. Furthermore, the President having closed the civil courts to the defendants, and military tribunals having by tradition no liking for restraint by civil courts, they were concerned lest the military trial be pushed to conclusion and the sentence carried out without giving notice and time that would permit a challenge to jurisdiction and a test in the Supreme Court.[18]

By steps too complicated for summary here the Supreme Court was reached by writs both of habeas corpus and of certiorari. From various parts of the country the justices rushed to Washington for a special term of the Court to hear this case only. They heard arguments on July 29 and 30, 1942, and on July 31 handed down a brief per curiam opinion to the effect that the charges alleged offenses that could be tried by a military commission, that the commission was lawfully constituted, and that the petitioners were lawfully held for trial. Apparently unimpeded by the swift action before the Supreme Court, the military commission and the President continued with the military proceedings, and for six of the saboteurs the death sentence was speedily executed.

A Supreme Court decision of such importance could not, however, be permitted to stand in the form of a mere per curiam opinion. From that time until the end of October, Chief Justice Stone and his colleagues wrestled with an opinion dealing with the issues more fully. Torn, on the one hand, between patriotism and the desire to show a united front in support of the administration in time of war and, on the other hand, dislike of the summary procedures of the President and the military, the Court gave to the public an opinion, in the name of the Chief Justice, that was far from clear and precise on some of the issues. True, it had no difficulty in distinguishing the present case from the Milligan case. The Milligan case had dealt with a civilian tried by a military tribunal. The current case, *Ex parte Quirin*,[19] dealt with members of the armed forces of the enemy who in violation of the law of war had engaged in military performance in and against the United States without wearing the uniforms the law required. As military personnel the saboteurs could therefore be tried before a military tribunal. But the Court dealt gingerly and, from the point of view of clarification of the law, most unsatisfactorily with the question whether the establishment of the commission and the secret and summary procedures of the commission, with review limited to the President, conformed to the Articles of War. Indeed, since the Court had found the commission to have jurisdiction, and since six of the defendants had already been put to death, the Court was now not in a position to quibble over past procedures. As for the contention that the President's proclamation and the status of the defendants as alien enemies prevented even this look into the proceedings by the civil courts, the Chief Justice so obscurely handled the justification of what the Supreme Court had done that the slap at the broad assertion of executive power was not widely perceived.[20]

3 In general the considered feeling of thoughtful people was and is that the Supreme Court, all things considered, took the right action with respect to the saboteur case. Approval is by no means as complete for its support of the military program for citizens of Japanese ancestry living on the West Coast—a topic briefly discussed in the preceding chapter. It is to be noted that the program for curfews, relocation, and internment was worked out largely by the military, partly

by officers on the Coast and partly by personnel in the War Department. In this situation, as in that of the saboteurs, military and popular sentiment was influenced by the shock of discovery of our unpreparedness and our tremendous naval loss at Pearl Harbor. The same kind of unpreparedness must not be permitted on the continent. There may have been intangible yearnings to restore self-respect by "making somebody pay" for our humiliating loss, even though those called upon to pay were for the most part inoffensive Americans who happened to have the same racial background as those who had destroyed our Pacific fleet. However that may be, Lieutenant General J. L. DeWitt, who was in charge of the Western Defense Command, determined to do something about the threat involved in the residence of large numbers of people of the Japanese race along the Coast, which was vulnerable both to attack from the sea and to sabotage of war industry. Unable to get the desired support from the Department of Justice, which was keenly aware of the constitutional rights of citizens as well as of the military danger, General DeWitt worked largely through the War Department in getting from the President the famous Executive Order No. 9066, in which the President, reciting the necessity for protection against espionage and sabotage, authorized the Secretary of War and military commanders designated by him

> to prescribe military areas in such places and of such extent as he or the appropriate Military Commander may determine, from which any or all persons may be excluded, and with respect to which, the right of any person to enter, remain in, or leave shall be subject to whatever restrictions the Secretary of War or the appropriate Military Commander may impose in his discretion.[21]

Because this sweeping order, although discussed primarily in connection with enemy aliens, applied to citizens as well, it was deemed advisable to get supporting legislation from Congress, legislation that would provide civil penalties for violation of military orders.[22] The measure was hastily passed, with apparently little realization of its implications for thousands of American citizens. The act provided for fine or punishment of persons entering, leaving, or remaining, in violation of military orders, in any area prescribed by military authorities. In effect it adopted as the law of the land such orders on this point as military commanders might prescribe in exercise of their military judgment.

Although military orders quickly prescribed curfews, evacuation, relocation, and internment, judicial tests came piecemeal. As previously discussed, the first Supreme Court case, decided June 21, 1943, involved directly only a curfew order for all persons of the Japanese race. Quoting in part the well-known phrase of Charles Evans Hughes that the power to wage war was the power to wage war successfully, the Supreme Court unanimously upheld the requirement, saying that

> Since the Constitution commits to the Executive and to Congress the exercise of the war power in all the vicissitudes of and conditions of warfare, it has necessarily given them wide scope for the exercise of judgment and discretion in determining the nature and extent of the threatened injury or danger and in the selection of the means for resisting it.

Under existing circumstances, "it is not for any court to sit in review of the wisdom of their action or substitute its judgment for theirs." [23] Limiting itself in this first case to discussion of the curfew order, even though it had unofficial knowledge of the entire program, which extended to the incarceration of citizens in relocation centers surrounded by military guards, the Supreme Court was able to avoid dealing with other activities until its decision in *Korematsu v. United States* [24] on December 18, 1944. Even here the Court limited itself as nearly as possible to a consideration of the validity of military orders evacuating Japanese-Americans from certain areas, treating the requirement of reporting to designated assembly centers as merely incidental. Here again, although with three justices dissenting, the Court upheld the exercise of the war powers.

It was only with the case of Mitsuye Endo, which tested the validity of holding an American citizen in a relocation center, that the Court placed a check on the government. This it did, not by a direct holding that the detention violated constitutional rights, but by holding that the statute and executive orders did not authorize the program. The Court, it is true, broadly hinted that the measures would be unconstitutional if they were held to authorize the detention, and two concurring justices insisted on saying so.[25]

The three Japanese removal cases brought no such utterances of defense of civil liberty as characterized the Milligan case of the Civil War period. Here, as far as constitutionality was concerned, the military was permitted to have its way. Justices Black and Douglas, who in nonmilitary situations usually took libertarian positions, were with the majority in the Korematsu case, and Justice Black wrote the opinion of the Court. Justice Douglas, it is true, wrote the opinion in the Endo case, holding detention to be unauthorized, but he dealt with constitutionality only by implication. The outright defenders of liberty were Justice Murphy, who might be expected to defend liberty in all but the most extreme cases, and Justice Roberts who had long been a critic of uncircumscribed executive power.

Important for a somewhat different reason was the opinion of Justice Jackson, who also dissented in the Korematsu case. More clearly than the other justices, Justice Jackson faced the predicament in which the judiciary finds itself in wartime. Whereas in postwar periods, as in the Milligan case, it can safely delineate limitations on the powers of the military, amid the confusion of war itself the courts may often have to choose between accepting military decisions that they find unpalatable and holding those decisions unconstitutional, after which they might suffer the embarrassment of having their decisions ignored—which was the experience of Chief Justice Taney in the Merryman case of the Civil War period[26]—or, in the doubtful event of their winning obedience, they might find that they had seriously interfered with the conduct of the war. None of the alternatives are palatable. Justice Jackson thought the majority had made a mistake in upholding civil enforcement of military orders that they were not competent to appraise.

> My duties as a justice as I see them do not require me to make a military judgment as to whether General DeWitt's evacuation and detention program was a reasonable military necessity. I do not suggest that the courts should have attempted to interfere with the Army in carrying out its task. But I do not think they may be asked to execute a military expedient that has no place in law under the Constitution.[27]

In other words, courts not being competent to appraise military performance, Justice Jackson would have kept the hands of the courts clean by refusing judicial interposition. Even in military situations where constitutional rights were involved, he would let the military have its way, since the subject matter was not appropriate for judicial review, but he would not corrupt constitutional law by giving judicial approval to military activities that the Constitution did not or might not sanction.

> A military commander may overstep the bounds of constitutionality and it is an incident. But if we review and approve, that passing incident becomes the doctrine of the Constitution. There it has a generative power of its own, and all that it creates will be in its own image. Nothing better illustrates this danger than does the Court's opinion in this case.[28]

Justice Jackson's position that the courts should look the other way with respect to military action taken during times of war, hoping in times of peace to restore civil protections to their pristine vigor, would make sense if we could assume, as we did in former years, that a state of war was the exception in our society and that peace was the persisting norm. But if war, or even what we call "cold war," is to provide the norm, and if the state of peace is to be the exception, then constitutional protections enforced by the courts may come to have little meaning for us. It may well be that we have ahead of us the formidable task of civilizing our military and bringing it more effectively within the restrictions of the Constitution, and of devising more effective use of the judiciary in connection with the military so that its function, even in time of war itself, will not be merely that of rationalizing what the military, operating exclusively in terms of its conception of military necessity, decides to do. But at best the task will require time and a great deal of hard work.

As for the Japanese removal cases specifically, it has been suggested that judicial alternatives were not as narrow as Justice Jackson defined them. Not all military commands were to be construed at the same level. An order for the discriminatory removal of citizens did not have to be treated as if it were an order for the deploying of troops. Here the facts involved were not technical military facts but were such as civilians could appraise at least as effectively as the military.[29] Furthermore, constitutionally speaking, we may assume that the basic mistakes here made were not the mistakes of the military, which, with its responsibility for coping with the enemy, might be expected to have some bias in disregard of the rights of citizens. The blame may well have lain primarily with the President and his civilian officers who phrased the Executive Order and with Congress which, instead of legislating directly on the subject, merely provided civil sanctions for military orders. If civil government is to be preserved free from military encroachment, the legislative and executive branches as well as the judiciary will have to refrain from making unjustifiable donations of civil jurisdiction to the military.

4 The Japanese removal cases differed from the Milligan case particularly in that they involved an intermixture of military and civil jurisdiction instead of jurisdiction that was purely military, and in that neither martial law nor the suspension of the privilege of the writ of habeas corpus was involved. Both the latter features were involved in *Duncan v. Kahanamoku,*[30] which tested the validity of military trials for civilians in Hawaii. In view of the shock and the demoralization created by the Japanese attack on Pearl Harbor it was but natural that the governor of the Territory of Hawaii should

proclaim martial law and suspend the writ of habeas corpus as authorized by the Hawaiian Organic Act, and that the President should give his approval to the Governor's action. Order was gradually restored on the islands, the American fleet in the Pacific was gradually built up, and the enemy was driven farther and farther to the westward. The military gradually permitted the restoration of the civil courts for civil functions but retained criminal jurisdiction for itself, even in matters having no direct military connection. As is usually true, its punishments were more severe than those likely to be prescribed in the civil courts.

The cases brought together in *Duncan v. Kahanamoku* involved offenses committed in 1944 when the enemy was far from Hawaiian shores. One of them had to do with embezzlement in a completely private enterprise and the other with a presumably energetic and courageous if foolhardy civilian who had assaulted two armed Marine sentries. Both offenders were given prison sentences by a military tribunal. On writs of habeas corpus the federal district court for Hawaii ordered their release on the ground that as of the time of their conviction a military tribunal had no right to try them, but the circuit court of appeals reversed that judgment.

The Supreme Court, in turn, reversed the judgment of the circuit court of appeals, and ordered the defendants released. Justice Black, as its spokesman, refused to say that the Constitution forbade the continuation of martial law and the military trial of civilians for civilian offenses after order had been restored in Hawaii, but he achieved approximately the same end by holding that the Organic Act of Hawaii must be read in the light of constitutional principles and must therefore be held not to authorize military trials under these circumstances. It was, indeed, the same pattern of indirection that he had followed in the Endo case. He implied an interpretation of the Constitution without asserting it.

> We believe that when Congress passed the Hawaiian Organic Act and authorized the establishment of "martial law" it had in mind and did not wish to exceed the boundaries between

military and civilian power, in which our people have always believed, which responsible military and executive officers had heeded, and which had become part of our political philosophy and institutions prior to the time Congress passed the Organic Act. The phrase "martial law" as employed in that Act, therefore, while intended to authorize the military to act vigorously for the maintenance of an orderly civil government and for the defense of the Islands against actual or threatened rebellion or invasion, was not intended to authorize the supplanting of courts by military tribunals.[31]

Justice Murphy challenged the several justifications offered by government counsel for the substitution of military for civil government and concluded:

The reasons here advanced for abandoning the "open court" rule of the Milligan case are without substance. To retreat from that rule is to open the door to rampant militarism and the glorification of war, which have destroyed so many nations in history. There is a very necessary part in our national life for the military; it has defended this country well in its darkest hours of trial. But militarism is not our way of life. It is to be used only in the most extreme circumstances. Moreover, we must be on constant guard against an excessive use of any power, military or otherwise, that results in the needless destruction of our rights and liberties. There must be a careful balancing of interests.[32]

Yet three justices thought the Court was going too far in the direction of devitalizing martial law. Chief Justice Stone concurred merely in the result, declaring that he did not think the term "martial law" as used in the statute was devoid of meaning, and Justice Burton dissented with the concurrence of Justice Frankfurter. Agreeing that the outer limits of military jurisdiction should be subject to judicial review, Justice Burton contended that possession of this judicial power obligated the courts to put themselves as nearly as possible in the place of those responsible for executive action.

For a court to recreate a complete picture of the emergency is impossible. That impossibility demonstrates the need for a zone of executive discretion within which courts must guard themselves with special care against judging past military action too closely by the inapplicable standards of judicial, or even military, hindsight. The nature of judicial authority is largely negative as contrasted with the generally positive nature of executive authority, and it is essential that the opportunity for well directed positive action be preserved and vigorously used if the Government is to serve the best interests of the people.[33]

He thought that the Supreme Court would not have granted the relief sought had it been requested at the time the offenses were committed, when the outcome of the war was still in doubt, and that it should not do so now by virtue of hindsight.

Altogether, in view of the multiplicity of opinions and the reliance of the majority of the Court on statutory interpretation rather than directly on the Constitution, the case told us little that was definite except that the authorities had exceeded the powers given by statute and that the two defendants were to go free. Here again we got no such illumination of constitutional principles as was afforded by the Milligan case after the Civil War.

5 From the trial of offenses committed by American civilians the discussion goes back to military trials of military and political agents of foreign powers. So gross and savage and ruthless were the offenses of enemy nations and their agents during World War II that public sentiment demanded punishment going beyond mere military defeat. With the most famous of all trials in this sphere, that conducted at Nürnberg to try the principal Nazi leaders, we have no concern at this point, for it did not involve action by our Supreme Court, apart from the fact that one member of the Court, Justice Jackson, was absent for many months while organizing and acting as a prosecutor in the trial. The involvements of the Supreme Court came rather from the Pacific theater. The first came in the form of its action on an application of the Japanese General Tomoyuki Yamashita for leave to file a writ of habeas corpus after he had been tried, convicted, and sentenced to death by an American military commission. The

conviction was for atrocities committed by forces under his command at the time when those forces were being disintegrated by victorious American forces. The conviction by a commission of five army officers came at the height of the surge of emotions accompanying the Americans' return to the islands from which they had been driven amid horrors such as Americans had not known since experiences with torture by American Indians. The defendant had the benefit of legal defense as provided by six other army officers who were also lawyers, but the trial was pressed to its conclusion so rapidly as to prevent adequate preparation of the case.

A majority of the Supreme Court, speaking through Chief Justice Stone in *Matter of Yamashita,*[34] denied the petition. The Court held that the military trial did not violate any provision of the Articles of War or any international agreement, and that the commission had the power to try the offense alleged. Jurisdiction having been determined, the Court, according to precedent, refused to inquire into the fairness of the trial conducted by the commission, such a commission not being a court whose proceedings were reviewable by the federal judiciary. The military was therefore left free to execute the sentence.

Although there is no evidence of likelihood that the dissenting opinions will mark the law of the future, the greater significance for our purposes may well lie in the earnest and indignant dissents written by Justices Murphy and Rutledge. Both of them contended that the guarantee of due process in the Fifth Amendment extended to all persons and to all adjudications of rights, whoever the persons might be. They contended that due process had here been denied in all respects except that of provision of counsel, and that the speed of prosecution in effect denied even this aspect of due process. In the language of Justice Murphy,

> No military necessity or other emergency demanded the suspension of the safeguards of due process. Yet petitioner was rushed to trial under an improper charge, given insufficient time to prepare an adequate defense, deprived of the benefits of some

> of the most elementary rules of evidence and summarily sentenced to be hanged. In all this needless and unseemly haste there was no serious attempt to charge or to prove that he committed a recognized violation of the laws of war. He was not charged with personally participating in the acts of atrocity or with ordering or condoning their commission. Not even knowledge of these crimes was attributed to him. It was simply alleged that he unlawfully disregarded and failed to discharge his duty as commander to control the operations of the members of his command, permitting them to commit the acts of atrocity. The recorded annals of warfare and the established principles of international law afford not the slightest precedent for such a charge. This indictment in effect permitted the military commission to make the crime whatever it willed, dependent upon its biased view as to petitioner's duties and his disregard thereof, a practice reminiscent of that pursued in certain less respected nations in recent years.[35]

Justice Rutledge also protested at great length and on many grounds, saying, with regard to the Fifth Amendment:

> Not heretofore has it been held that any human being is beyond its universally protecting spread in the guaranty of a fair trial in the most fundamental sense. That door is dangerous to open. I will have no part in opening it. For once it is ajar, even for enemy belligerents, it can be pushed back wider for others, perhaps ultimately for all.[36]

Certain it is that if the civil courts are to participate in the necessary process of civilizing the military as the military comes to occupy a more intimate place in our lives than ever before, there is no evidence that the majority of the Supreme Court was here concerned with playing such a civilizing part.

The Supreme Court faced another difficult decision in *Hirota v. MacArthur,* which involved motions for leave to file petitions for writs of habeas corpus by Japanese political and military leaders who had been tried and convicted by the International Military Tribunal for the Far East—an international tribunal similar to that which operated at Nürnberg—and who were being held for punishment by General Douglas MacArthur as Supreme Commander for the Allied powers. Justice Jackson preferring not to participate because of his recent connection with the Nürnberg trials, the eight justices divided four to four on whether to hear arguments in the case. In favor of hearing them were Justices Black, Douglas, Murphy, and Rutledge, and voting in the negative were Chief Justice Vinson and Justices Reed, Frankfurter, and Burton. Rather than have it announced to the world, including the Oriental part of it, that Japanese leaders had been put to death with four justices doubting the legality of the proceedings, Justice Jackson joined the group asking that arguments be heard, hoping that treatment of the case on its merits would permit him to withdraw again.[37] The argument took place, after which a majority of the Court held that the power of habeas corpus did not extend to a military tribunal that was primarily international in character, even though the Supreme Commander in charge of the defendants was an American general. Justice Murphy dissented, but did not present an opinion, perhaps out of deference to the point that division might have a bad effect on American standing in the Orient. Justice Rutledge reserved decision, and Justice Jackson did not vote. The Court stated its position in a brief per curiam opinion.[38] With what might be important implications for the future, Justice Douglas wrote a concurring opinion to the effect that since General MacArthur was acting as an American general as well as an international commander, an American court might inquire by habeas corpus into the legality of his detention of the prisoners. He found, however, that they were legally held in the exercise of political rather than judicial power.

6 The several cases here discussed dealt bit by bit with the scope of the privilege of the writ of habeas corpus when the jurisdiction of military tribunals was challenged. The Quirin case demonstrated the right of alien enemies tried and held in the United States to habeas corpus inquiry. The Yamashita case demonstrated essentially the same right, since the Philippines were at that time American territory. Inquiry was refused in the Hirota case, not because the parties were enemy

aliens but because the tribunal was not one over which the United States had jurisdiction. The question was therefore left to be determined whether habeas corpus inquiry could be instituted in an American court to determine the legal status of persons tried abroad by an American tribunal and held in a foreign prison. The question became increasingly important with the extent of American occupancy and operation in foreign countries. During the years immediately following World War II, motions for leave to file petitions for habeas corpus on behalf of German enemy aliens who had been tried and punished by American tribunals in Germany were filed in the Supreme Court in large numbers and were denied.[39]

The constitutional question was partly clarified by *Johnson v. Eisentrager*,[40] decided in 1950, in a case which had come up through the lower federal courts in such a way that the Supreme Court could hardly avoid taking a position. A group of German officers, who in conjunction with the Japanese had continued fighting against the United States in China after Germany had surrendered, were tried and convicted by an American military commission in China for violation of the laws of war and were sent to occupied Germany for imprisonment. The officers sought by habeas corpus to challenge the right of the military commission to try them. The district court for the District of Columbia dismissed the petition, but the court of appeals for the District reversed the decision, holding that the petitioners were entitled to judicial inquiry.

The Supreme Court, voting six to three, held that alien enemies tried before an American military tribunal and imprisoned abroad had no such right to judicial inquiry. Justice Jackson, speaking for the Court, carefully distinguished between the rights of alien enemies and those of American citizens, without deciding whether American citizens tried abroad under similar circumstances would have had access to habeas corpus inquiry. Admitting that aliens in the United States who had enemy status had some rights in our courts, Justice Jackson noted by contrast that "the nonresident enemy alien, especially one who has remained in the service of the enemy, does not have even this qualified access to our courts, for he neither has comparable claims upon our institutions nor could his use of them fail to be helpful to the enemy." [41]

But here again the pattern of civil-military relations and of executive-judicial relations is highlighted as much by the dissenting opinion as by the opinion of the Court. Justice Black, with the concurrence of Justices Douglas and Burton, contended that the privilege of habeas corpus review should extend anywhere people were held by American authorities, not to determine whether decisions as to punishment were rightly made but to decide the narrower question whether, as in this case, "the military tribunal was legally constituted and whether it had jurisdiction to impose punishment for the conduct charged." [42] He contended that our constitutional mandate of equal justice under law should be applied as well when we occupy lands across the sea as when our flag flew merely over thirteen colonies. He concluded by saying:

> Habeas corpus, as an instrument to protect against illegal imprisonment, is written into the Constitution. Its use by courts cannot in my judgment be constitutionally abridged by Executive or by Congress. I would hold that our courts can exercise it whenever any United States official illegally imprisons any person in any land we govern. Courts should not for any reason abdicate this, the loftiest power with which the Constitution has endowed them. [43]

While the Black argument was written only in dissent, it should be remembered that the problem of adequate supervision of the behavior of American armed forces and other agencies operating abroad has not been solved, and that we may yet have to adopt the Black expedient of giving the judiciary that minimum of power necessary to determining the authority of American agencies to do what they do do in specific instances, with respect to both the people of the land in which our agencies operate and American citizens located there. There is cogency in the argument that American judicial power of inquiry should be available wherever agencies of American government operate, however far from home they may be and however alien and hostile the people affected by their conduct.

7 At this point the story shifts back to the scope of the power of the military to try civilians for offenses in some way connected with the activities of the military. The Uniform Code of Military Justice,[44] adopted by Congress in 1950, provided for military trials not only for members of the armed forces and the civilian contingents of those forces but also for honorably discharged service personnel, for offenses alleged to have been committed during their periods of military service, and, under certain circumstances, for the dependents of military personnel, for offenses committed while accompanying such personnel in foreign countries. The provision with respect to former service personnel was written into the Uniform Code without the approval of at least some of the military personnel then exercising jurisdiction in such matters. The Judge Advocate General of the Army protested against it before a congressional committee, saying:

> I believe this is unnecessary and the inevitable result will be public revulsion against its exercise. It has been my experience that no matter how just and fair the system of military justice may be, if it reaches out to the civilian community, every conceivable emotional attack is concentrated on the system. I recognize that . . . many serious offenses committed by persons subject to military law are not detected until the person is separated from the service. I do not advocate that such persons should go unpunished. I merely suggest that you confer jurisdiction upon Federal courts to try any person for an offense denounced by the code if he is no longer subject thereto.[45]

In spite of the plea to "save the military from a lot of unmerited grief," [46] the provision was not deleted.

Test of the provision came in 1953 when Robert W. Toth, honorably discharged from the Air Force, was charged with premeditated murder committed during his service in Korea and was flown to Korea for military trial. His sister filed a petition for a writ of habeas corpus in the district court for the District of Columbia, and he was brought back for the hearing and was ordered released. The circuit court of appeals reversed this order. Thereafter the Supreme Court twice heard arguments in the case, and by a vote of six to three held that the military could not constitutionally try a civilian for an offense committed earlier when he had military status. The petitioner, the Court held, was entitled to all the procedures and protections of a civil trial. Congress could provide for civilian trials by conferring jurisdiction upon federal courts. The power of Congress to regulate the armed forces, said Justice Black,

> does not empower Congress to deprive people of trials under the Bill of Rights safeguards, and we are not willing to hold that power to circumvent those safeguards should be inferred through the necessary and proper clause. It is impossible to think that the discipline of the Army is going to be disrupted, its morale impaired, or its orderly processes disturbed, by giving ex-servicemen the benefit of a civilian court trial when they are actually civilians.[47]

Yet three justices lamented this curtailment of congressional power to provide for punishment of offenses, noting that Toth's alleged accomplices who remained in the service had been punished by military courts whereas he went free. Two of the three justices went so far as to contend that a man with an honorable military discharge was not a "full-fledged civilian," but had a "conditional discharge only," to the extent of his continuing responsibility to the military for any crime he might have committed while in the service.[48] On the whole, in spite of the majority of two justices on the side of curbing military jurisdiction to this limited extent, the trend of judicial attitudes was by no means clear. One group put emphasis predominantly on the side of traditional constitutional rights and the other on the side of the adequacy of military power. Neither group took an absolutist position with respect either to power or to rights, but the shadings of difference were enormously important. A slight change in situation and a shift or two in the membership of the Court might have a profound effect upon the development of the law.

Illustration of the ease with which the Supreme Court balance might be shifted came with two decisions in June, 1956, dealing with the power of the military to try two wives of servicemen, each of whom had resorted to the drastic expedient of killing her husband. Under the Articles of War, civilians employed in direct connection with the military services had long been subject to the same summary forms of trial that applied to military personnel itself, but extension of this power to civilian wives connected with the military only through their marital status was a contribution of the Uniform Code of Military Justice of 1950. The question of policy, as Congress must have seen it, or would have seen it had it given extensive thought to this single item of the Uniform Code, was a difficult one. Civilian wives and other dependents, like civilians generally when abroad, could be left to trial by foreign courts when they committed offenses in foreign lands. Such arrangements might have worked reasonably well in England and other countries with legal procedures not greatly different from our own, although there was always the unpleasant possibility that the trials might reflect the dislike of local people for the American military and add to the severity of punishment. In countries very different from our own, as in some where theft is punished by amputation of a hand, members of Congress would revolt at accepting foreign justice.

It would have been possible to vest American federal courts, or a federal court in the District of Columbia or somewhere else in the United States, with jurisdiction in such cases, and to bring the defendants home for jury trials with all the protections guaranteed by the Constitution. But it would have been difficult to provide for transportation of enough witnesses and records to give juries a clear understanding of cases.

Another option was suggested by the case of *In re Ross*,[49] decided in 1891. By treaty with China the United States had secured the right to try, in its own consulates in China, American citizens who had committed offenses in that country, who but for the treaty would have been subject to punishment by China pursuant to Chinese laws. With respect to the civilian dependents of American military personnel abroad, it might have been possible to work out treaties or executive agreements with foreign countries for their trial before special courts analogous to consular courts. Agreement with the country in question was necessary, indeed, to enforce jurisdiction in the military trials provided for by the Uniform Code of Military Justice. The special courts, like consular courts, would have had to operate without jury trial and other expedients required in the courts of the United States, but the military element would have been eliminated.

But Congress permitted the Uniform Code to stand as drafted, as far as military trials for civilian dependents abroad were concerned, and the Supreme Court, in the light of the Toth case, discussed above, had to decide whether the two women, tried and convicted abroad by American military tribunals and returned to the United States for imprisonment, had been denied constitutional rights in being subjected to military trial. Five justices found that trial by military tribunals was not unconstitutional. Three justices dissented, promising to write opinions for filing at the ensuing term, and Justice Frankfurter wrote at considerable length in criticism of the opinion of the majority, written by Justice Clark, but postponed taking his own position.[50]

Justice Clark used the Ross case in support of his position that Congress could use abroad what are called "legislative" courts for the trial of American civilians without the benefit of many of the procedural protections given to defendants at home. Since Congress could provide for such trials it seemed to him that, for the dependents of military personnel, it could use the courts of the military for its purpose. He placed the holding of the Court against its factual background as follows:

> In the present day we, as a Nation, have found it necessary to the preservation of our security to maintain American forces in some sixty-three foreign countries. The practical necessity of allowing these men to be accompanied by their families where

> possible has been recognized by Congress as well as the services, and the result has been the creation of American communities of mixed civilian and military population at bases throughout the world. In all matters of substance, the lives of military and civilian personnel alike are geared to the local military organization which provides their living accommodations, medical facilities and transportation from and to the United States. We could not find it unreasonable for Congress to conclude that all should be governed by the same legal standard to the end that they receive equal treatment under law. The effect of a double standard might well create sufficient unrest and confusion to result in the destruction of effective law enforcement.[51]

Yet the decisions did not settle the constitutional question or even determine finally what should happen in these particular cases. Before the minority could file their opinions at the term of the Court beginning in October, 1956, Justice Minton, one of the majority of five in these cases, announced his intention of retiring and did retire, to be replaced by Justice Brennan. Over the opposition of Justices Reed, Burton, and Clark (with Justice Brennan not participating), the Court decided to rehear arguments in the cases. Before the reargument took place, in March, 1957, the size of the majority was further reduced by the retirement of Justice Reed. His successor, Justice Whittaker, was not chosen in time to enable him to participate in the cases, so that decision was left to eight members.

Although the rehearing had the effect of bringing about the release of the two women,[52] it had little effect in clarifying the law. No opinion had the support of a sufficient number of justices to be labeled the opinion of the Court. At one extreme, Justices Clark and Burton adhered to the position they had taken a year earlier. At the opposite extreme, Justice Black won the adherence of Chief Justice Warren and Justices Douglas and Brennan in rejecting the argument of the Ross case and other cases indicating that the United States might try civilians anywhere in the world without giving the full protection of the Fifth and Sixth Amendments. Justice Harlan, who had been of the original majority, and Justice Frankfurter, who in the previous year had not been able to make up his mind in the time available, concurred merely in the 1957 decision that these civilian dependents charged with capital offenses could not be tried by the military. Each added a long opinion to the opinions of Justices Black and Clark, but none of the opinions clarified the situation. So it is that development of law in this field is still in progress, with civil and military jurisdictions still overlapping in bewildering fashion.

Because basic determinations are still in the process of being worked out, it is of course impossible to offer a precise summary. In general it may be suggested that military justice is gradually growing more humane—with important legal revisions following the Civil War, World War I, and World War II—and that directly or indirectly it permeates more and more deeply into civilian life. We are a long way from the position, attributed to General William Tecumseh Sherman of Civil War fame, that "it will be a grave error if, by negligence, we permit the military law to become emasculated by allowing lawyers to inject into it principles derived from their practice in the civil courts, which belong to a totally different system of jurisprudence."[53] Even though the primary purpose of military trials is still that of securing obedience rather than weighing precisely the issues of justice in individual cases, a great deal of the procedure of civil justice has found its way into the Uniform Code of Military Justice. On the other hand, the trial of civilian dependents of American military personnel stationed abroad indicates directly the permeation of the military into civilian areas. Also significant, though harder to characterize, is the permeation of civil government with military personnel, retired or otherwise, and the importation into civilian processes of modes of thought and action that are in varying degrees hostile to the regime of safeguarded operations that has been dominant in our tradition. It remains to be seen to what extent we shall bring about a marriage between the two systems, and which of the two the progeny will most resemble.

8 In conclusion, it is well to revert to the subject treated at the beginning of our discussion, namely, the war powers of the President as the source of enhanced powers in the executive branch of the government. During World War II the Supreme Court interfered not at all with the exercise of the powers claimed, and it cannot be contended that there has been any appreciable curtailment since that time. However, the check placed on President Truman in the Steel Seizure case of 1952 is worthy of note as illustrating the power of the Court in this sphere when it sees fit to exercise it. At that time we were engaged in war in Korea—or in a police action, if such it is to be called. The date had been set for a strike in the steel industry as a result of an unresolved wage dispute. The President directed the Secretary of Commerce to take possession of most of the steel mills and keep them running. The executive order, reciting the military emergency and the need for uninterrupted steel production, was justified "by virtue of the authority vested in me by the Constitution and laws of the United States, and as President of the United States and Commander in Chief of the armed forces of the United States. . . ." The Supreme Court—to state briefly what was held in a series of opinions some of which were very long—held by a vote of six to three that the President did not have the power to seize the industry either by virtue of anything said in the Constitution or in the statutes or by virtue of his status as President or commander in chief of the armed forces.[54] No doubt was expressed that Congress could have given the power to the President, and opinions differed as to the extent to which the President was here inhibited merely by the fact that there were statutes empowering him to follow other procedures than those here adopted. At any rate, if the presidential office had inherent power to act in the absence of federal legislation, it was held not to have such power in the light of the fact that Congress had prescribed other modes of seizure that might in other circumstances be used.

But whatever the line of reasoning followed by Justice Black as official spokesman of the Court, or by Justices Frankfurter, Douglas, Jackson, Burton, and Clark in concurring opinions, or by Chief Justice Vinson dissenting for himself and Justices Reed and Minton, the essential fact, for our purposes, is that the Court drew a line to limit the executive power of the President, or rather that the Court held that there was such a line and that President Truman had crossed it. The Constitution, said Justice Black for the Court, refuted the idea that the President was to be a lawmaker. In Congress, and not in the President, was vested the power to make the laws that the President was to execute. However, because of the brevity of the opinion called the opinion of the Court and the length and diversity of the other opinions, little light is thrown on the question whether the Court in the future will be able to discover and enforce a line of jurisdiction that the President may not cross. So it is that we are left in doubt as to the scope of presidential war powers as well as the scope of the power of the military in relation to the exercise of civil judicial power. The law, indeed, is in a state of ferment rather than a state of fixity.

V *Race and the Constitution*

Notwithstanding our commitment in the Declaration of Independence to the position that "all men are created equal, that they are endowed by their Creator with certain unalienable rights, that among these are life, liberty and the pursuit of happiness," the American people have been slow to admit that men of all races were entitled to enjoy equal rights within the territory of the United States. We have contended that aliens generally had no right to come to the United States except as we chose to welcome them, and that aliens already here had no right to remain if we saw fit to expel them. Among aliens seeking admission we have felt free to pick and choose in terms of the lands from which they came, and until as late as 1952 we have made race a basis for discrimination among those upon whom American citizenship might be conferred. The legal questions involved have been many and complicated, and the Supreme Court has had to work out in this field a diverse group of difficult constitutional decisions.

1 As we have already dealt piecemeal with the predicament in which Japanese on our West Coast found themselves during World War II, even when they were American citizens by birth, it seems well to begin with the constitutional position of Orientals in the United States rather than that of Negroes, which must inevitably occupy most of our attention here. During the first century of our life as a nation when the federal government did little to regulate the flow of immigration, the states with port cities were restive at the arrival of strange peoples, whatever their racial backgrounds, and sought in various ways to regulate immigration at the ports of entry.[1] The early concern with Oriental immigration was primarily on the West Coast. In California, where Chinese began to arrive in considerable numbers soon after the Gold Rush of the early 1850's, the new arrivals were welcomed at first but soon began to stir enough competitive hostility to bring restrictive legislation as well as group persecution. In 1862 the legislature passed "An Act to Protect Free White Labor Against Competition with Chinese Coolie Labor," which the state supreme court held in violation of the federal Constitution.[2] Measure after measure came thereafter to protect white residents from the influx of Chinese, who were willing to work hard for low wages and were able to live with a frugality white laborers would have found intolerable.

California measures restricting the rights of Chinese gave rise to cases drawing the line between the police powers of the state, on the one hand, and on the other hand the equal protection of the laws which the Fourteenth Amendment guaranteed to all persons. This was particularly true with regard to measures in which San Francisco sought to protect its homes and business establishments, built largely of wood, at once against ravaging fires that at times created wholesale disasters and against worker competition from Chinese laborers who carried on much of the laundry business of the city, usually in flimsy wooden structures. The constitutional line was hard to draw, for the legitimate and illegitimate motives were thoroughly mixed.[3]

Political pressure from the Western states led in 1880 to modification of the existing treaty with China to enable the United States to exclude Chinese coming as laborers, but the new treaty did not affect the rights of Chinese already here to remain, or to return to the United States after visiting in their homeland. Congress passed the permitted legislation and then, on the ground that new immigrants were entering the country on the false claim that they had been here before as legitimate immigrants, abruptly closed American ports to returning Chinese who did not bring with them certificates entitling them to re-entry, certificates that they could not bring for the reason that none had been issued at the time of their departure. The Supreme Court nevertheless upheld the act of Congress, in spite of the violation of the treaty.[4] Chinese laborers continued to be smuggled into the United States. To cope with this evil Congress provided for deportation of aliens of the Chinese race unless they secured from a government official a certificate of residence. The certificate was to show that the alien was legitimately here at the time of the passage of the act and was to be issued only after identification by "at least one credible white witness." Many Chinese in the United States lived only among their own people, spoke only their own language, and knew no white witnesses, whether credible or not. The Supreme Court nevertheless upheld the measure.[5] To its credit, however, the Court drew the line at another provision of the same act that authorized imprisonment without judicial trial of Chinese found by an administrator to be unlawfully in the United States.[6]

It should perhaps be said that the relevant acts of Congress did not reflect any basic hostility on the part of the United

States toward the Chinese people. It marked the conviction, merely, that Chinese laborers, however worthy as people, should remain in their own country, and that the territory of the United States belonged to the primarily Caucasian peoples who had first settled the country. Caucasian Americans were deeply concerned about invasion, however peaceful, by the millions of people living in the overpopulated Asiatic countries. Their attitude was one of "America for Americans," with Americans defined as primarily Caucasian except for the Negro population whose presence here was predominantly the responsibility of Caucasians. People born in the United States were of course citizens, whatever their race, and were entitled to remain here as part of the body politic, but it was felt that Orientals were so different from Caucasians that they were in a deep sense "unassimilable," and that we ought to be careful not to add to their numbers in this country.

As Chinese immigration was brought under control, immigration of workers from Japan also became critical. Control there was achieved first by "gentleman's agreement" and later by statute. Even so, the number of Orientals in some of the Western states was great enough to stir hostility and bring discriminating legislation. Because of their race, neither Japanese nor Chinese could become naturalized. Until 1870, indeed, only free white persons could be naturalized. At that time sentiments growing out of the North-South conflict brought an amendment to permit naturalization of aliens of African birth and African descent,[7] but the privilege was not extended to other races. Chinese and Japanese were therefore "aliens ineligible to citizenship." Japanese were particularly successful as market gardeners. To prevent them from holding land, a number of Western states forbade the ownership or leasing of land by aliens who had not taken the initial steps toward becoming citizens. Since the Orientals in question were ineligible to citizenship, they naturally could not take these initial steps.

The Supreme Court held that although the Constitution protected all persons, and not merely citizens, against state discrimination with regard to the right to engage in all lawful callings, the situation was different when it came to the ownership or control of agricultural land. "The quality and allegiance of those who own, occupy, and use farm lands within its borders are matters of highest importance, and affect the safety and power of the state itself." [8] Since in this area a state could discriminate between citizens and aliens, it could also discriminate between those who by lawful procedure had declared their intention to become citizens and those who had not—whether the latter were restrained by lack of desire or lack of legal opportunity.

Restrictions in the name of race on the right to naturalization gradually crumbled. In 1940 the right was extended to descendants of races indigenous to the western hemisphere. In 1943 it was extended to Chinese, our allies in the war. In 1946 it was extended to Filipinos and persons of races indigenous to India. At the close of the war, however, Japanese aliens still remained ineligible. As Japanese aliens, along with American citizens of Japanese ancestry who had been held in relocation centers or scattered throughout the country, returned to the West Coast to resume their lives there, Californians attempted to prevent the aliens from getting around the ban of its land law. When an alien bought a small tract in the name of his infant citizen son, expecting to operate it himself in the name of his son, the state seized the land. In *Oyama v. California* [9] the Supreme Court held that the infant son of the alien had the same right to own land as did any other infant citizen, and that the California law denied him equal protection of the laws.

California also attempted postwar discrimination against aliens ineligible to citizenship, which by this time meant principally Japanese, by denying them fishing rights in coastal waters that they had had before the war. While admitting that the state had the right under earlier decisions to conserve its internal natural resources by limiting their exploitation to citizens, the Supreme Court held that the California statute which dealt with fish moving back and forth between coastal waters and the deep sea could not be classified as a conservation measure. It recognized the statute for the discriminatory measure that it was, and found it a denial of equal protection of the laws.[10]

The end of racial discrimination on the basis of ineligibility to citizenship came in 1952 when Congress eliminated race as a barrier to naturalization. It came without the development of any clear-cut statement of principle. In general the assumption seems to be that, for those representatives of non-Caucasian races who are here, there must be equality of opportunity with regard to naturalization and the granting of privileges generally. But the policy with regard to immigration is to grant the major quotas to the nationals of countries that are already most extensively represented here, and thereby to promote assimilation into one vast social group. The Supreme Court participates very little as far as immigration is concerned but does become extensively involved with the guarantee of rights to aliens on our shores and to their citizen offspring and to those who become naturalized. In that area it seems to have performed its task of protection well in recent years, if one excepts the period of World War II when, as it is apt to do in time of war, it bowed to the allegations of military necessity.

2 The earliest experience of the Supreme Court in connection with race problems was of course with American Indians, whom Caucasian explorers and settlers found here, and with Negroes whom they brought, largely as slaves. The Indian story, for all its historical involvements, is pretty much a finished story and will not here receive much attention. American Indians are citizens of the United States, and they are entitled to all the rights and privileges conferred by the Constitution. Such litigation affecting them as reaches the Supreme Court has largely to do with disputes over titles to property, in which it appears they are as fully protected as are white people, with whom they more and more intermingle and intermarry. Dwindling flickers of discrimination showed,

it is true, in a case decided in 1954 involving the right of a widow to bury her deceased Indian husband in a cemetery where such burial was prohibited by a restrictive covenant. The widow, who had bought a cemetery lot, brought suit for damages because of the exclusion but failed because an Iowa court accepted the restrictive covenant as valid. The Supreme Court divided four to four on the contention that the state court had denied equal protection of the laws, and then, finding that Iowa had thereafter outlawed such restrictive covenants, decided that certiorari in the case had been improvidently granted.[11]

It seems clear, however, in spite of Supreme Court refusal to interfere to right a wrong in this individual case, and indeed partly from the opinion in that case, that discrimination of this and other kinds against American Indians is on its way to an end. Indeed, both from the point of view of constitutional rights and, whether for the good of the Indians or not, from that of racial identity, the remaining minority group of American Indians seems likely very soon to become merged completely with the mass of the American people who are largely European in origin.

3 However regrettable our experience in relation to Orientals and American Indians, it is in relation to Negroes that our experience has been ugliest and most unfortunate. When the American colonies were still the colonies of European powers, it became a profitable business to kidnap Negroes in their African homeland and bring them to America as slaves. Slavery, although it was nowhere mentioned in the Constitution by name, was obliquely recognized as a lawful institution, and Congress was forbidden to prohibit the importation of slaves before 1808, twenty years after the Constitution was expected to go into effect. The institution, economically profitable in the South, or at any rate believed to be so there, but in general not profitable or important in the North, marked one of the rival issues between the two regions. The rivalry showed itself early in the admission of new

states to the Union, each region being concerned with how admissions would affect the balance of power in the federal government. From the early 1830's onward most of the problems of American federalism, including those that led to Supreme Court decisions, were considered in part in the light of the sectional conflict. The story is long and complicated and can be told here only in terms of the highest of its highlight features, of which the first in this abbreviated statement may be said to be the famous case of Dred Scott.

Seldom in American history, we can say in preface to that story,[12] has the name of a man as inconspicuous as Dred Scott become so well known to millions, both in his own time and in future decades. Dred Scott was a Negro, a Negro slave, and from the scanty historical records it would appear that he was quite ordinary in that capacity. No record indicates outstanding intelligence or any burning desire to better his own position or the tragic position of his people or to take revenge on their masters. We have no evidence of fervor in the efforts he made to purchase his freedom and that of his family, or of more than amused interest in the stormy litigation carried on to determine his right to freedom. He was not the victim of martyrdom or even of ultimate frustration, for he achieved freedom through manumission after the attempt by litigation had failed.

No, this inconspicuous old Negro laid down no claim to fame except for one fact. That fact was that he lent his name to litigation that became far more important than the fate merely of this one man and his similarly enslaved family. We know little of the origins even of the name he lent. It is said that during his early years he was labeled not sonorously, and in some undefined sense ominously, as *Dred* Scott but by the ordinary name of Sam.[13] We are tempted to wonder, indeed, whether the case name of *Sam Scott v. Sandford* would have stirred the American people as did the one we know so well. However that may be, what concerns us is that he gave his name to a case that embodied all the boiling fury, the frustration, the rage, the indignation, and the vibrant idealism that had long been building over the issues of slavery. Dred Scott, then, as we have known him, was not so much a Negro or a man as the name of a case, of one of the most fateful cases in American history. That case is important to us one hundred years after its decision partly, of course, because it echoes problems of race relations that are still dramatically with us, for all their change in form. But it is important also for the light it sheds on the character and processes of American government, and particularly on the position of the federal judiciary among the three branches. It is with this topic most directly in mind that the story of the decision and the suggestion of later parallels will be presented.

In recalling the story of the Dred Scott decision to those to whom details may have grown dim, it is worth emphasizing that the point actually decided by the Supreme Court was a narrow one, and that strictly speaking, it did not extend beyond the technical realm of judicial procedure. The Supreme Court decided merely that the circuit court of the United States in Missouri, in which the case had originated, had not had jurisdiction to hear and decide it. The case was important primarily because of things said beyond the range of those actually necessary to support this finding. In deciding the jurisdictional question the Supreme Court calculatedly managed to speak with judicial authority on the major political issues that were tearing the country apart, that were leading to the "irrepressible conflict." Judicial opinions, the majority favoring the position of the proslavery South and the minority favoring the antislavery North, became instruments in the growing political battle. When a judge speaks officially he speaks in the name of the law, and his words carry a weight not derived from other positions in officialdom. The Supreme Court speaks in terms of the law of the Constitution, the "supreme law of the land," which to thoughtful people then as now carried overtones of natural law, the law of fundamental rightness derived from a judgment higher than the minds of men. The Supreme Court, in other words, when it spoke in terms of the Constitution, spoke also with the overtones of deity. And whereas deity as voiced by a minority of two of the justices spoke in behalf of Dred Scott and the power of Congress to exclude slavery from the territory, as voiced by the majority of seven and in the language of the Chief Justice it left Dred Scott in slavery and denied the power of Congress to interfere with the "peculiar institution" of the South.

In spite of the doctrinal abuses that are at times practiced in the name of natural law, and in the name of constitutional law treated in a natural-law vein though the word "natural" is not employed, the American people have always had higher-law leanings and a reverence for that something "higher" which the Constitution represents. Furthermore, we have tended to agree upon the fundamentals of our constitutional and higher law, in their embodiment of the practices of democracy and the principles and devices of procedural justice. We have in general accepted the courts as the appropriate interpreters of that which was constitutional and also "higher." But we have never reached agreement as to where the line is to be drawn between the things that are constitutional and higher, and those that are mundane and subject to determination by the political process. We have always resented it—or when on the losing side, we have always resented it—when judges, speaking in Jovian language of things higher, used the judicial process to give a spurious sanctity to one side of what ought to have been treated as a purely political controversy, to be settled through the political branches of the government. Furthermore, when particular decisions have offended us, it has been hard for us to believe that they belonged in the higher realm where the judiciary had the final say, rather than in the more earthy realm of practical politics.

What the Supreme Court did in the Dred Scott case was to take up multiple issues of the status of Negroes, and the power of Congress over that status, which had been and were the focal points of stormy political controversy. Some of the issues, as already indicated, could have been avoided in determining the rights of Dred Scott in this case, but the majority of the Court attempted to settle them politically as well as judicially, by imprinting on the proslavery position the sanctity of a Supreme Court decision in a matter of constitutional law. The fact that the majority did just that is not modified—indeed it is illuminated—by the fact that they were goaded to that action by the determination of two minority justices to use the forum of the Supreme Court to give sanctity to the opposite position.

The goal of abolitionist sentiment in the 1850's was to use the federal government, the instrument of the Constitution, to free the enslaved Negroes wherever possible and to give them protection as persons and citizens. Northern and Southern agitators whipped the country into a furore of agitation. President-elect James Buchanan announced privately: "The great object of my administration will be, if possible to destroy the dangerous slavery agitation and thus restore peace to our distracted country." [14] The Supreme Court attempted to quell that agitation by denying constitutional power on behalf of the Negro. At the time of the adoption of the Constitution, said Chief Justice Taney, Negroes had been regarded as "so far inferior, that they had no rights which the white man was bound to respect." [15] They were not included in the term "citizens" as that term was used in the Constitution.[16] They could be held as property, and an act of Congress denying property rights in Negroes taken into United States territories "could hardly be dignified with the name of due process of law." [17] Such, he contended, had been the original meaning of the Constitution. The Constitution did not change with public opinion.

> It is not only the same words, but the same in meaning . . . : and as long as it continues to exist in its present form, it speaks not only in the same words, but with the same meaning and intent with which it spoke when it came from the hands of its framers, and was voted and adopted by the people of the United States.[18]

It is a commonplace fact of history that neither the unnecessary pronouncements of the Supreme Court nor the feeble efforts of President Buchanan brought peace to the "distracted country," and that the decision stimulated further the agitation it had been designed to quell. On the issue of slavery a major portion of the country rejected the Supreme Court as the spokesman of its higher law. "The name of Taney," proclaimed the abolitionist Senator Charles Sumner, after the Civil War and after Taney's death, "is to be hooted down the page of history. . . . An emancipated country will fasten upon him the stigma which he deserves. . . . He administered justice at last wickedly, and degraded the judiciary of the country, and degraded the age." [19]

The great lesson of the Dred Scott case lies not in determination of whether the Court was right in its interpretation of the Constitution: it lies in the conclusion that when the people are fundamentally divided on basic issues, the judiciary will act at its peril if it intervenes unnecessarily to impose a judgment of higher law in support of one political faction and to aid in the defeat of another. Here the Court not only failed of its purpose but saw its efforts used to enhance the very controversy it sought to terminate. It saw a war waged and constitutional amendments adopted to nullify its interpretation. It brought discredit upon itself for many years to come. Far better for the Court had it adhered to its original plan of avoiding the basic questions by holding, as it had done in an earlier case,[20] that the status of a slave within a slave state was determined by the laws of that state, and that the courts had no basis for interference with that status in the fact that for a time the slave had resided in free territory. The questions involved were questions still in political controversy. Constitutional language was indefinite, and public opinion had not yet arrived at the degree of unanimity that permits of settlement in terms of principles of higher law.

4 As a judicial phenomenon the shadow of the Dred Scott decision projected itself across the war years to reproduce oddly similar configurations in the reconstruction period. The peace that President Buchanan could not achieve came only

after military repression had proved secession impossible—with a partly reconstituted Supreme Court following the trail of the military to hold that a state could not constitutionally leave the Union.[21] The "Radical" Congress set out to recapture power lost to the President during the war, to nullify the Dred Scott decision as to issues of citizenship and slavery, to protect itself against the return of Southern aristocracy to power in the federal government, and to ensure protection of newly freed Negroes against oppression by their former masters. The amendments abolished slavery, defined and guaranteed rights of both state and national citizenship, forbade the states to deny privileges or immunities or due process or equal rights against racial discrimination, and closed in each instance with the provision that Congress should have power by appropriate legislation to enforce the provisions of the article.

Many studies of the records of the adoption of the amendments, and of discussion of them in connection with supporting legislation, have attempted to show what specific clauses of the amendments were intended to mean.[22] The picture, however, remains confused. The pulling and tugging of diverse interests brought modification of phraseology but little evidence as to clear intent. After the amendments were adopted, the legislators who had participated in their adoption, and those who succeeded them, sought to make the amendments mean what they wanted them to mean—as other statesmen had done with the original Constitution. As the zeal of the war years dissipated, statesmen turned more and more to political and economic problems other than those of slavery, and the drift of motivation had its effect on what was said about the meaning of the amendments.

Without attempting to add to the studies of this subject, it is worth noting that the Congressmen who framed the amendments were at that time reasserting congressional power against both the President and the judiciary. They came close to ousting President Johnson from office, and they watched with threatening eyes the handling of cases in which the Supreme Court might have declared the Reconstruction Acts unconstitutional. Their interest, to repeat, was in congressional power. It is also worth noting that, concerned though they were about preserving the Union as a federal system, they adopted the three amendments largely to take power and discretion away from the states, because they distrusted the states in the specified areas.

The Supreme Court, on the other hand, came into the picture without any institutional commitment to the Negro and with a kind of traditional commitment to the Constitution, in which, as the Court had been applying it for three quarters of a century, broad powers were left to the states. Concerned as it was with leaving protection of the great body of civil rights in the hands of the states, it is not surprising that the Supreme Court, in the Slaughter-House Cases [23] in 1873, by a vote of five to four virtually nullified the Fourteenth Amendment provision that "No state shall make or enforce any law which shall abridge the privileges or immunities of citizens of the United States." The fact that the protection sought in this case was for white businessmen and not for Negroes evidently impressed the majority of the Court with the extent to which the clause, if broadly interpreted, might transfer from the states to the federal courts the broad protection of civil rights. By its decision the Court blocked such a transfer.

The Slaughter-House Cases left yet to be determined the meaning of the due process and equal protection clauses of the Fourteenth Amendment and the clauses at the end of each of the three amendments that gave Congress the power by appropriate legislation to enforce the provisions of the articles. The fact that Congress immediately enacted statutes to protect Negroes against violence demonstrated the contemporary belief that it had power under the amendments to pass the laws necessary to make the over-all purpose effective. Yet in Congress itself some members interested in getting back as quickly as possible to normal government argued that the amendments stood primarily as prohibitions on the states, and that the enforcement provisions did not empower Congress to legislate substantively on civil rights, but merely to provide machinery for defeating prohibited state action. Justice Joseph P. Bradley, a newly appointed member of the Supreme Court, picked up this argument. In 1874 in a lower federal court where white men were on trial under the Enforcement Act of 1870 for the massacre of Negroes in Louisiana, he held that Congress had exceeded its powers in legislating generally to protect civil rights.

> The power of Congress, whether implied or expressed, to legislate for the enforcement of such a guaranty, does not extend to the passage of laws for the suppression of ordinary crime within the states. This would be to clothe Congress with power to pass laws for the general preservation of social order in every state. The enforcement of the guaranty does not require or authorize Congress to perform the duty which the guaranty itself supposes it to be the duty of the state to perform, and which it requires the state to perform. . . .[24]

Without fully asserting the Bradley position, the Supreme Court affirmed the lower court decision. In the meantime, in 1875, Congress passed the last of its measures to implement the postwar amendments in behalf of the Negro. The Civil Rights Act of that year sought to guarantee to Negroes equal accommodations in inns, public conveyances, and places of amusement. The Department of Justice had to undertake enforcement of the act in a period of growing disillusionment with reconstruction. Reconstruction governments proved inefficient and corrupt; proponents of white supremacy in the South fought on, resorting to violence and intimidation and passive resistance to reconstruction machinery; and Northern leaders grew weary of the effort and turned their attention from Negro welfare to the business problems of the new era. The political compromises of 1877 and the election of Rutherford B. Hayes to the presidency resulted in the withdrawal of federal troops from the South and the collapse of what remained of the reconstruction effort.[25] The drift provided the worst possible atmosphere for enforcement of the Civil Rights Act. When in 1883 the Supreme Court passed on the constitutionality of the statute, Justice Bradley, its spokesman, carried with him all but one of his colleagues in finding the statute unconstitutional. In what are known as the Civil Rights Cases he held that the Fourteenth Amendment was merely prohibitory upon the states, and that the implementing legislation Congress was empowered to enact included only measures to counteract forbidden laws enacted by the states. It did not extend to substantive legislation for the protection of civil rights.

A brief quotation from the Bradley opinion shows it as but a judicial ratification of the conviction widely held among white people that enough time had been spent in getting protection for the former slaves and that they must now find some way of getting along without special attention:

> When a man has emerged from slavery, and by the aid of beneficent legislation has shaken off the inseparable concomitants of that state, there must be some stage in the progress of his elevation when he takes the rank of a mere citizen, and ceases to be the special favorite of the laws, and when his rights, as a citizen or a man, are to be protected in the ordinary modes by which other men's rights are protected.[26]

There is little doubt that the Bradley opinion reflected the dominant sentiment of the times. With the exception of the Negroes themselves and a minority of faithful friends, the people were tired of giving special protection to the former slaves. It was felt to be time for the return to power of the dominant factions in the several communities. The Supreme Court, at the moment in tune with the times, did not encounter an outpouring of public indignation as it had done after the Dred Scott decision. It had identified the higher law with current public sentiment, and could count on current public approval for its action.

But in one important respect the Civil Rights decision closely resembled the Dred Scott decision. The Dred Scott decision had set up bars to federal action in an important field, bars that could be removed only by constitutional amendment, in an area where constitutional language was not clear and where public sentiment was divided, and the Civil Rights decision set up similar bars. Here likewise constitutional language was unclear. And although public sentiment at the time was more in harmony with the decision, the field was one of political issues about which public sentiment might well change, as it has done in some degree, leaving the judicial prohibition as a barrier against democratic achievement of political purpose. In other words, the mood of disillusionment and weariness with protection of Negro rights proved too ephemeral to serve as an adequate basis for a statement of constitutional law.

It is not here asserted that Congress in the 1880's was obligated to enact legislation to protect Negro rights in the face of opposition from the electorate. That point can be left for speculation or discussion elsewhere. Certainly it would have been completely constitutional for Congress to repeal the Civil Rights Act of 1875. Congressional repeal could have been followed by congressional re-enactment if and when public sentiment changed. But what we got was in effect repeal by judiciary, in terms such that Congress was thereafter barred from enacting a similar measure, however much it and the people might at some future time desire such legislation.

It is true, of course, that the constitutional question was decided by the overwhelming majority of eight to one, and that such weight of opinion is entitled to respect. Yet the dissenting opinion of Justice Harlan as read today sounds plausible in its statement that "the substance and spirit of recent amendments of the Constitution have been sacrificed by a subtle and ingenious verbal criticism." [27] Justice Harlan emphasized the fact that the Fourteenth Amendment was not merely prohibitory upon the states, as the majority had implied. Its first clause was positive, creating and granting both state and federal citizenship. That which the Constitution created could be protected by Congress as well as by the judiciary, against all comers and not merely against the states. He advanced also this narrower argument:

> In every material sense applicable to the practical enforcement of the 14th Amendment, railroad corporations, keepers of inns and places of amusement are agents or instrumentalities of the state, because they are charged with duties to the public, and are amenable in respect of their duties and functions, to governmental regulation.[28]

Racial discrimination by these agencies was therefore in effect discrimination by the states, and could be dealt with by Congress through such legislation as was necessary to provide a real remedy.

However that may be, the majority of the Supreme Court not only disposed of the Civil Rights Act of 1875 but also removed from Congress in future years any sense of obligation it might otherwise have developed for enactment of broad civil rights legislation by holding that it had no such constitutional power. As a result, gradual changes in public sentiment in favor of protection of the rights of the Negro have found their limited expression not through Congress, where political matters should be given their fullest consideration and where the democratic process is in the main supposed to be worked out, but rather in the executive and judicial branches. While the decision in the Civil Rights Cases had no such adverse effect on the prestige of the Supreme Court as the Dred Scott decision, which was nullified by war and constitutional amendment, the Civil Rights decision brought about a farther-reaching impediment to the protection of Negro rights.

5 The Dred Scott and Civil Rights decisions were approximately only a quarter of a century apart, and were linked by the intervening war and its aftermath. After three additional quarters of a century during which the country has been only incidentally preoccupied with race relations, we look back over the hundred years to see whether the handling of the Dred Scott issues has parallels in the judicial decisions of today or provides lessons or points warnings for the United States in the 1950's. Our minds quickly span a series of de-

cisions which, variously, protected the political rights of Negroes by upholding federal statutes regulating elections and outlawing state electoral abuses, protected the procedural rights of Negroes in many kinds of court actions, and enforced as to substance as well as procedure the requirement of equal protection of the laws. But what immediately arrests our attention is the series of cases dealing with discrimination in education and related fields, culminating in the decision in *Brown v. Board of Education* and in the generalization that "Separate educational facilities are inherently unequal." [29] Our interest, in the light of Dred Scott, is in whether the Supreme Court in the 1950's is rigidifying into fundamental law positions on which both public opinion and public law may and perhaps ought to change, and whether the Court is exercising power that ought to be exercised by the political branches of the government.

The answer, it may be said at once, is by no means as clear as it was in the Dred Scott case or in the Civil Rights Cases. Positions taken hereafter, therefore, will be only suggested and not asserted confidently. It is to be noted that the position on segregation taken in the Brown case with respect to elementary education, and in immediately preceding cases with respect to collegiate and professional school education, only recently became the unanimous position of the Court. As late as 1939, when in *Missouri ex rel. Gaines v. Canada* [30] the Court outlawed discrimination in law school education, Justice McReynolds, joined by Justice Butler, presented in significant language the resulting alternatives with which the state seemed to him now to be faced: "She may abandon her law school and thereby disadvantage her white citizens without improving petitioner's opportunities for legal instruction: or she may break down the settled practice concerning separate schools and thereby, as indicated by experience, damnify both races." [31]

The next nine years, covering World War II with its intermingling of races in employment and in the armed services, brought great changes in public attitudes and in the personnel of the Supreme Court. No member of the Court now believed that desegregation would "damnify" both races. Yet some or all members sensed the bitterness of the attack likely to be directed at the Court if the "separate but equal" doctrine of *Plessy v. Ferguson* [32] were abandoned and segregation found to deny equal protection of the laws. Among justices inclined to widespread expression of judicial opinion on important issues, it is as if an advance agreement to act unanimously on segregation matters had been entered into to give a beleaguered Court the full advantage of a united front. By good fortune or by virtue of behind-the-scenes guidance, segregation cases came before the Court in such a way as to permit it to lead up gradually to the ultimate issue. When in 1948 in *Sipuel v. University of Oklahoma* [33] the Court passed on Oklahoma's exclusion of a Negro from its law school, it used but some two hundred words of a per curiam opinion to hold that the case was governed by the Missouri decision. When in the same year in *Shelley v. Kraemer* [34] the Court held that judicial enforcement of restrictive covenants with regard to sale of property to Negroes likewise violated the equal protection clause, the justices were similarly reticent, speaking exclusively through the opinion of Chief Justice Vinson.

In other cases in the field of segregation the justices continued to speak only through the Chief Justice. It was Chief Justice Vinson who in 1950 in *McLaurin v. Oklahoma State Regents* [35] announced that equal protection was denied to Negroes in a state university when they were segregated within classrooms, libraries, and cafeterias. On the same day he spoke for a unanimous and otherwise silent Court in *Sweatt v. Painter,*[36] holding that a Negro was denied equal protection of the laws by being excluded from the University of Texas Law School, even though the state provided a separate law school for the benefit of Negroes. Counsel in this case had argued not only that there was inequality between the two law schools but that discrimination was inevitable under the "separate but equal" formula. Among other presentations on behalf of Negroes, it may be significant that counsel for the American Jewish Committee, another powerful minority group subject to various types of discrimination, filed a brief as friend of the Court to assert that the separate but equal doctrine was a "fiction that must be pierced" and that segregation was by definition unequal.

Finding actual inequality between the two law schools, the Court noted a reservation of judgment as to whether the "separate but equal" doctrine was still in good standing. This reservation stood as an indirect invitation to a challenge of the doctrine in other cases. The finding of unconstitutional inequality, furthermore, even where separate law schools were provided for people of different color, and the analysis of that inequality in such a way as to demonstrate that it would be very difficult to segregate and still provide equality, led to challenges to segregation in the even more sensitive field of elementary education. As we all know, the group of cases headed officially by the Brown case was argued before the Supreme Court at great length in December, 1952. At the end of the term the Court returned the case to the docket for reargument, asking for discussion of a series of questions about the intent of the framers of the Fourteenth Amendment concerning segregation in the schools, the intent of the Congress that submitted the amendment, the intent of the ratifying legislatures and conventions, the power of Congress or the judiciary under the amendment to interfere with segregation, whatever the original intent had been, and the nature of the decree to be issued if the judiciary was to outlaw segregation.[37] The question showed the Court aware of the Constitution-making elements of its task and of the difficulty of issuing enforceable decrees in effect forbidding a negative—that is, forbidding states to refrain from educating colored and white children in the same schools.

Following the death of Chief Justice Vinson, the reargument took place in December, 1953, with Chief Justice Warren at the helm. The unanimous decision, voiced again through the Chief Justice, though through a different man, came in May, 1954, with restoration of the cases to the docket for still further argument about the kind of decree to be entered. It is with this basic decision in 1954 that we are here primarily concerned rather than with that of 1955 remanding the cases to the courts of original jurisdiction with directions to issue decrees and enforce compliance "with all deliberate speed." [38] The Court found the evidence inconclusive as to whether those involved in adoption of the Fourteenth Amendment had had any intention with respect to segregation in education. The decision was based neither on the history of the amendment nor on precise textual analysis but on "psychological knowledge" of "public education in the light of its full development and its present place in American life throughout the Nation." [39] On such important but at the same time highly evanescent grounds, segregation in public education was found to constitute a denial of equal protection of the laws, and, in the companion case of *Bolling v. Sharpe* [40] in the District of Columbia, a denial of due process of law.

6 Apart from noting that the principle of the Brown case has been extended to public recreation, public housing, and public transportation, further analysis of cases or of the process of enforcement is not here the primary purpose. Our concern, rather, is with the projecting shadow of the Dred Scott decision, in which the Supreme Court went beyond the strict necessities of the case to a disastrous attempt at settlement of issues more properly left to the working out of the political process, which has greater flexibility. We note in the Brown case some of the absoluteness apparent in the Taney opinion in the Dred Scott case and in the Bradley opinion in the Civil Rights Cases. An example is the statement, quoted above, that "Separate educational facilities are inherently unequal." [41] Such inherent inequality would not be found in separating the first grade from the second grade, or elementary schools from high schools, or high schools from colleges. It would not be found in separating males from females, in spite of the implications of the Nineteenth Amendment. Presumably it would not be found in separating classes within the same grade in

terms of ability, even though in some communities such separation might result at least temporarily in grouping most Negro children in the lower sections.

No, for all the widespread discrimination that has taken place against Negroes through the segregation process, it is not segregation or separation that is fundamental. What is fundamental is a conviction pegged to color, and all too often unconsciously held by Negroes as well as white people, that color, and particularly black color, carries with it a stigma of inferiority. The conviction is steeped in a tradition brought by early immigrants from foreign lands and is rooted in the pattern of one-time enslavement. The pattern of enslavement had to be "justified" by some kind of doctrine in order to allay the sense of guilt of the kidnapers of free Negroes and the possessors of slaves. To a degree it had to be justified even in the minds of the Negro victims, in order to make possible their acceptance of degrading treatment that they could not escape and that, without some kind of justification, would have been intolerable. In modern terminology, they were "brainwashed" into seeing themselves as inferiors and as rightly treated as slaves; and although some among them rejected the classification and were always on the point of rebellion, in most of them the label of inferiority was so deeply imprinted that it carried over from generation to generation as a part of the cultural heritage.

To a tragic extent the heirs of both the slaveholders and the slaves have carried in their systems the conditioned responses of the slave culture. As to the former, we have examples in the current resistance to integration in the face of the highest judicial pronouncement, and in such materials as the vitriolic attacks made on the Supreme Court after the Brown decision, preserved for years to come in the Appendix to the *Congressional Record.* In the descendants of former slaves we also find continuing evidence of the earlier conviction of inequality. We find it, for example, in the conduct of those who overcompensate by aping the misbehavior of oftentimes unadmirable white people. In some colored people we find it also in a sensitive and critical area wherein lies danger to the Negro race as a race. The pounding insistence generation after generation on the superiority of white people over black has so impaired the sense of personal and racial worth among some of the victimized people as to lead to the measurement even of feminine charm, by both men and women, in terms of Caucasian rather than Negro racial characteristics. The Negro race will be in danger until it fully recaptures a sense of its own independent worth and of an equality that can be confidently asserted without obsequiousness and without brashness. The conviction of inequality, whether held by Caucasians or Negroes, is the source of the basic threat to equality in government and to the equal protection of the laws.

Our immediate governmental responsibility, therefore, is to provide the conditions of formal legal equality over the succeeding decades, while unjustified convictions of inequality are gradually being dissipated; to do what government can do to dissipate those feelings while remembering that there are depths to which government cannot go without violating the realms of privacy that our democracy is committed to protect; and to see to it that what might ordinarily be legitimate action is not made an instrument for denial of constitutional rights. It is a responsibility to be fulfilled in the midst of grinding social pressures, and it requires maximum flexibility for achievement. We sense, indeed, a crying need for the flexibility of the political process as distinguished from the relative rigidity of the judicial process, and we can deplore the fact that the Supreme Court in the Civil Rights Cases of 1883 relieved the congressional conscience by freeing it of major responsibility. Perhaps more relevant to the public need at the time of the Brown decision would have been the overruling of the Civil Rights decision rather than of *Plessy v. Ferguson* with its "separate but equal" doctrine. But the Supreme Court of today has no means of overruling the Civil Rights decision unless Congress goes in the face of that decision and enacts a statute in violation of it.[42] This, we currently see, Congress is most reluctant to do. If a majority is ready to enact the mild and limited civil rights program endorsed by the President, it seems unwilling to eliminate from Senate procedure the obstruction of the filibuster, which stands in the way of broad and effective action in the liberating spirit of the post-Civil War amendments.

What we need, in other words, is a flexible legislative program that can change with changing experience—experience that in some areas might possibly include adequate action by individual states—in addition to, if not in place of, judicial edict, which may in some instances prove too rigid in spite of the flexibility of the equitable mandate of "deliberate speed." The fundamental-law principle of equality is there for all to see and for phrasing by the judiciary, but the delineation and enforcement of equality is too complicated to be achieved by the judicial negative alone.

Implicit in what is being said here, but not essential to the central thesis, is the doubt whether, under different circumstances, separate educational facilities would necessarily be "inherently unequal." There is of course no doubt that the instrument of segregation is currently made a highly effective instrument of inequality. To the extent to which the Supreme Court decision is made effective, we have eliminated an instrument of inequality by outlawing that instrument for all time, whether or not under other circumstances inequality might be produced. The time may well come, even though at a distant day, when Negroes will feel such assurance of their own equality as themselves to prefer segregation in education and recreation, particularly where adolescent generations are concerned. Legislative solution, perhaps led by an active and responsible executive, might be able to provide desirable flexibility. Judicial fiat almost inevitably decrees a rigidity that is likely to embarrass.

In any event, the warning lesson of the Dred Scott case remains with us. Although in the determination of points necessary to be decided we need from the Supreme Court the articulation of our highest constitutional ideals, we do not need from it a straining after solutions that can appropriately come only through the political process. A vital assumption of our constitutional system is that we operate as a democracy. Leadership in constitutional development must come through the legislative and executive branches. In the decision of cases the judiciary must refine, restrain, and harmonize, but it cannot safely take over the task of leadership without threat of disaster both for itself and for the country. Conversely, the people cannot solve their political problems, the problems calling for creative democratic activity, by themselves neglecting those problems and juggling for solution by judicial pronouncement. The judiciary can be the servant to democracy and a tremendous aid in the consolidation of democratic achievement, but it can never serve as a replacement of democracy itself. This generalization holds true with respect to race problems, whatever the race that gives rise to them, and with respect to constitutional problems generally, whether or not issues of race are involved.

VI *The Goal of Judicial Endeavor*

From a widely ranging discussion of the Supreme Court's handling of important groups of cases, we turn now to more precise pinpointing of the central function of Court performance, to the goal of judicial endeavor as far as this particular tribunal is concerned. We have previously quoted Justice Cardozo to the effect that diligence and memory and normal powers of reasoning might suffice where the judicial function was imitative or static, but that "The travail comes when the judicial function is dynamic or creative." [1] The function must be dynamic or creative when situations are novel and when precedents, although providing hints or clues, fail to function as authoritative commands.

During the past quarter of a century constitutional precedents have been peculiarly ineffective as authoritative commands, in situations that have called for the maximum of creativity on the part of statesmen in all fields. With wars and depressions and economic inflationary booms, with changing internal patterns of social and economic life and changing patterns of international relations, the judiciary, like the legislative and executive branches of government, has been in travail.

1 As we watch Court performance under extremes of strain it is easier to outline factors that, however important, do not constitute its central function than to say what that function is. For example, although the work of the Court is done through the decision of cases, it is in no sense to be measured by the number of cases decided. Indeed, in spite of the constitutional crises of recent years, the number of cases decided annually with written opinions has declined by approximately half since a quarter of a century ago. An indication of the importance of the quality of judgments, as compared with quantity, is reflected in the following statement by Justice Frankfurter written in 1943:

> The judgments of this Court are collective judgments. Such judgments presuppose ample time and freshness of mind for private study and reflection in preparation for discussions in conference. Without adequate study there cannot be adequate reflection; without adequate reflection there cannot be adequate discussion; without adequate discussion there cannot be that mature and fruitful interchange of minds which is indispensable to wise decisions and luminous opinions.[2]

Quality is more important than bulk or numbers—a point on which presumably all justices would agree. There must of course be quantity as well as quality but, within reason, the latter must come first.

Again, the central function of the Court is not the protection of property, in spite of the importance of property and business as basic to the structure of our society, and in spite of the tendency of justices of earlier generations to equate the laws of property with the laws of God. Property, it is true, must be protected, but it must be protected as an instrument for the achievement of welfare, and not identified with that welfare itself—and the protection must come from all branches of the government and not merely from the judiciary. Here we can agree with Justice Jackson who, in his posthumously published book of lectures, criticized a "judicial activism" on the part of the pre-Roosevelt Court, which treated the protection of property virtually as its goal in a judicial crusade against the forces of socialism.[8]

But if the Court is not a specialized instrument for protection of property against society and against other branches of government, we may question also whether its central, as distinguished from an incidental, function is to operate as a trouble-shooting organization for the protection of liberty against the same sources of attack. Again with Justice Jackson, we can question whether proper guidance is offered by what he calls a "cult of libertarian judicial activists," who would have the judiciary maintain dominance over other branches of the government where issues of liberty are concerned. In a sense we are here challenging the theory of the primacy of liberty, about which much has been said in recent years and which was discussed earlier. Our purpose is not to cast reflection on the importance of liberty; it is not merely to suggest that the protection of liberty cannot be left to judges in black robes, any more than to knights in shining armor, but must be the function of our democracy as a whole. It is rather to point out that, particularly in view of the fact that the protection of liberty, like the protection of property, is but partially in the hands of the Court and is but an incident in the total compass of judicial responsibility, the protection of liberty must not be permitted to distract judicial attention from a still broader and more comprehensive purpose.

Furthermore, in terms of the discussions in Chapters IV and V, we can say that the function of the Court is not centrally that of finding the place of the military or of keeping the military in its place, or of assuring to minority races, even belatedly, the protections the Constitution affords them. Vitally important as are these responsibilities, they are shared by other branches of the government and by the people at large, and, beyond that, the Court, with its multiple responsibilities unifying into a kind of organic whole, must not become too fully preoccupied with them. And certainly, notwithstanding the importance of the separation of powers and the federal relationship and other devices of our constitutional system, we cannot say that the Court is there primarily as a watchdog over particular mechanisms and practices. In this field again the several branches and agencies of government and the people at large share the responsibility that is only incidentally the responsibility of the Supreme Court.

It is worth repeating that in the search for the central function of the Supreme Court we must see it in the context of the government as a whole. We must see its dependence on the President for the selection of its personnel and on the appropriate agencies of the executive branch for its protection and the enforcement of its orders. We must take into account its dependence on Congress for appropriations to pay its expenses, for legislation providing for its establishment and prescribing its jurisdiction, and for the body of federal law that the courts will be called upon to enforce. Although the Court has some specific protections in the Constitution, such as those providing for life tenure and preventing reduction in salary, it cannot be regarded as in any high degree divorced from the other branches of the government.

This being true, the Court, for all its supposed aloofness, cannot be regarded as completely separated from the populace. We do not have to resort to ridicule with the charge that the Court follows the election returns to make the point that what the other branches of the government do to and about the Court will depend in considerable part on what the people want done. It takes a considerable amount of popular pressure to secure a constitutional amendment such as that nullifying the Court's decision in the Income Tax cases. It takes a deep sense of public need, and not merely the leadership of a dynamic President, to secure enactment of a program like the New Deal program, whose enforcement made a vast difference in the career of the Court and gave rise to or accented many of the problems discussed in this book. The Court, in other words, must operate in a governmental and popular context already provided for it, and it cannot hope to escape from that context.

Within its governmental and popular setting, the judiciary as a whole, as distinguished from the Supreme Court in particular, has the peculiar responsibility for the decision of cases, for the settlement of disputes within the framework of the law and by way of the judicial mechanism as we have developed it over centuries of Anglo-American legal history. It does not, it is true, possess the total of the judging function, for tasks of adjudication belong to the legislative and executive branches as well, and are carried on at times by mechanisms that differ from the orthodox courts principally in name and hardly at all in organization and operation. The fact remains, however, that the adjudication of central and basic issues under the Constitution and under statutes falls primarily to the judiciary, and that the judiciary is the agency of government devoted exclusively, or almost exclusively, to adjudication.

All branches of our government, it is true, and not merely the judiciary, are concerned with law. They are concerned with finding its meaning as well as with making it, changing it, and carrying it into effect. And yet in the American tradition it has always been peculiarly true, in the language of Chief Justice Marshall already quoted, that "It is emphatically the province and duty of the judicial department to say what the law is." [4] However careful our reading of constitutions and statutes, we have had the feeling that we knew the law only when we had it through official judicial interpretations. It has been almost, indeed, as if there were no law, but only the potentiality of law, until judges articulated, or "found," its interpretation. Writing in 1913 about attitudes toward law during the latter half of the nineteenth century, Roscoe Pound stated:

> It should not be forgotten . . . that we have been a law-ridden people. Nowhere else in legal history has so much been committed to the courts nor have courts been relied upon so completely for the practical conduct of government as in the United States after the Civil War. By the last quarter of the nineteenth century, nearly every phase of public as well as of individual activity had come to be subject to judicial review. We had developed the common-law doctrine of supremacy of law to its furthest logical conclusion and we were wont to refer to limitations running back of all constitutions which even sovereign peoples were bound legally, not merely morally, to observe.[5]

Although Dean Pound was concerned about the deviation from reliance on the courts in the twentieth century, a trend that has continued at a growing pace in recent years, the quotation suggests the essence of the judicial function.

2 It is of course true that the closer we come to the core of the judicial process the greater becomes the difficulty of characterization, and the more we see multiplicity of ingredients. Deeply embedded is the belief in the operation of the variously defined something called right reason, whether it be considered the instrument of the mind only, as divorced from things emotional or religious, or whether it be regarded as a manifestation of the laws of the Supreme Being. For all our disillusionment with the behavior of courts in particular instances, we continue to expect of them, in general, better-reasoned performance and a deeper probing of righteousness, with less preoccupation with narrow expediency and considerations of mere power than are to be found in the other branches of government. We expect judges to be learned in the law and to possess integrity and balance and wisdom. In varying degrees, but in a particularly high degree in the federal system, we protect them as to salary and tenure and give them surroundings calculated to minimize external pressures on them. While knowing that they cannot be and should not be completely divorced from their times, we try to make possible an atmosphere in which "righteous" men with learning and disciplined reasoning powers can best exercise their pow-

ers in the decision of cases. Once they are appointed, we tend to treat our judges as if they had the capacity and the motivation to deliver what we seek from them. Since judges are human, it is of course possible for them to become intoxicated with their self-importance, to take on an air of spurious sanctity and to be themselves deluded by it—to become devotees of "The Cult of the Robe," to use the figure employed by Jerome Frank.[6] It may be necessary at times to deflate a particular individual, or an entire court, or perhaps even to chastise an entire profession through public criticism. Yet we tend to believe that we get most nearly what we want, from others as well as ourselves, if we make our expectations articulate and display adequate faith in their fulfillment. To put the matter another way, there is more prospect of approaching an ideal if we expect the ideal to be attained than if we assume from the beginning that attainment or even approximation is impossible.

3 Our concern here is of course not so much with the judiciary as a whole as with appellate courts, and particularly with the Supreme Court. Such illumination of the judicial process as the justices provide is provided largely through their judicial opinions, which must be read in the light of the contexts of particular cases and not treated as aloof discussion of great universals. Although a considerable minority of the justices have written books of one kind or another and published articles on diverse subjects, the works of Justice Cardozo, written while he was Chief Judge of the New York Court of Appeals, mark the only outstanding contribution to jurisprudential analysis. Even the monumental works of Justice Story, written more than a century ago when our institutions were less well defined than they now are, were concerned much more with showing what the law was than with analysis of its inner content. The contributions of individual justices come most often as flashing passages developed in connection with particular cases and embedded in opinions not necessarily otherwise notable. In spite of the loss of under-

standing that is involved in taking passages from their contexts, it seems well to illustrate here from the work of many justices the diversity of individual syntheses that may be collected from the mass of materials in the *United States Reports.*

Chief Justice Marshall, in addition to stressing the judiciary's special responsibility for declaring the law, highlighted judicial responsibility for giving the Constitution its rightful place as the supreme law by the warning: "we must never forget that it is a constitution we are expounding." [7] He revealed his own absolutist thinking and that of his times through the generalization: "the power to tax involves the power to destroy." [8] Chief Justice Taney revealed the impact of a social philosophy on decisions through the assertion: "While the rights of property are sacredly guarded, we must not forget that the community also have rights." [9] Chief Justice Waite phrased a limitation on judicial power in the assertion: "For protection against abuses by legislatures the people must resort to the polls, not to the courts." [10]

Justice Holmes, colorful phrase-maker on many subjects, revealed a conception of the Constitution as more fluid than rigid in such comments as: "the word 'liberty,' in the Fourteenth Amendment, is perverted when it is held to prevent the natural outcome of a dominant opinion," [11] and "The power to tax is not the power to destroy while this Court sits." [12] Justice Brandeis posted a warning concerning the use of reason in the judicial process through his assertion: "If we would guide by the light of reason, we must let our minds be bold." [13] Justice Van Devanter found criteria for judicial measurement of state action in the degree of its consistency "with the fundamental principles of liberty and justice which lie at the base of all our civil and political institutions and not infrequently designated as 'law of the land.' " [14] Justice Cardozo measured the indispensability of judicial procedures in terms of whether they were "of the essence of a scheme of ordered liberty." [15] Justice Roberts explained that the function of the Court in passing on an act of Congress was to "lay the article of the Constitution which is invoked beside the statute which is challenged and to decide whether the latter squares with the former," and to "announce its considered judgment upon the question." [16] Justice Stone stressed the need for judicial self-restraint,[17] warned against "tortured construction of the Constitution," [18] and issued the reminder that "Courts are not the only agency of government that must be assumed to have the capacity to govern." [19] Justice Sutherland asserted that "The check upon the judge is that imposed by his oath of office, by the Constitution and by his conscientious and informed conviction," and that he had "the duty to make up his own mind and adjudge accordingly." [20] Justice Black denounced use by the judiciary of what he called the natural law formula and declared that it "should be abandoned as an incongruous excrescence on our Constitution." [21] Justice Frankfurter, who defended natural law reasoning,[22] admitted, however, that the powers of the Supreme Court were "inherently oligarchic," [23] and contended that since the power of the Court was merely the power of negation over governmental measures, "the indispensable judicial requisite is intellectual humility, and such humility presupposes complete disinterestedness." [24] Chief Justice Vinson, warning that constitutional provisions did not stand in isolation one from another, declared: "To those who would paralyze our government in the face of impending threat by encasing it in a semantic strait-jacket we must reply that all concepts are relative." [25]

The items quoted above are but samples of many of their kind that can be found scattered through the more than three hundred fifty volumes of opinions. As fragments they suggest and illuminate the nature of the judicial process, but nowhere do they provide a synthesis on the subject. Without undue reliance on any one of them or on any incomplete collection, we permit them en masse to form a mosaic from which derives much of our understanding of the judicial function and of the goal toward which the judiciary strives.

4 There is value, furthermore, in going beyond individual judicial utterances that are remembered merely as such to

phrases and the articulation of categories that, although not expressed in the Constitution, have been picked up from individual or group utterances and used as formulas or guides of varying degrees of definiteness for rationalizing future decisions. Some of them seem to retain virtually permanent validity. Others give way in the face of changing attitudes and are limited to narrow spheres of use or are abandoned altogether. Among them we may list the following:

Police power
Political question
Business affected with a public interest
Fair return on a fair value
Separate but equal
Stream of commerce
Rule of reason
Clear and present danger (with the even less definite "manifest tendency" test)
Primacy of civil liberties

In our pursuit of the goal of judicial endeavor it is worth while to explain these judge-made categories more at length. The concept of the police power of the states was evolved more than a century ago to highlight those generally local powers the states might continue to exercise even though their exercise touched matters that might lie also in the areas of interstate and foreign commerce which Congress had the power to regulate. The concept continued in use after the adoption of the Fourteenth Amendment to define areas where the states might regulate in spite of the inhibitions of the due process clause, and particularly with respect to the regulation of the use of property. A body of definition of police power gradually evolved, embracing powers for protection of health, safety, public morals, and public welfare. The time came, indeed, when the states, instead of being regarded as the repositories of powers not granted to the federal government and not denied by the Constitution, were regarded pretty much as the possessors of police power only, with non-police power delegated to the federal government or denied altogether.

The concept is still in good standing, with more in the way of content than it possessed a third of a century ago.

The concept of political questions was also utilized more than a century ago to mark constitutional questions that could be decided only by the political branches of the government, the legislative and executive branches, and not by the judiciary. This device also is still in good standing; it enables the judiciary to avoid determining questions it is ill equipped to determine or that could be settled in any event only with the effective support of the political branches.

The concept of business affected with a public interest came into use in the so-called Granger Cases of 1877 to label businesses that, because of the closeness of their relation to the state, might be regulated as to rates and prices in spite of the prevalence of the laissez-faire principle, then being read into due process of law, that prices were in some way sacred and immune from regulation. Here, as in connection with police power, the tendency developed to list as affected with a public interest primarily those businesses that in past decisions had been held to be so affected. When in 1934 the Supreme Court abandoned this reliance on precedents and held that any prices might be regulated if the public interest was found to require it, the category lost most of its importance for constitutional law.

The concept of fair return on a fair value, read into constitutional law in 1898, was used to mark the limit of the power to regulate prices when the government, whether state or federal, possessed the power in some degree. It gave rise to an enormous amount of litigation because of the indefiniteness of both "fair return" and "fair value," with use in new cases of the body of precedent developed in earlier cases. With the coming of the New Deal period and the period of World War II, the Court gradually abandoned the concept and held that government might regulate if necessary to do so for the public welfare, whether or not the regulation left the opportunity to earn a fair return on a fair value.

The concept of separate but equal was articulated just before the turn of the present century when it was held that in making facilities available to people of different races, a state did not violate the equal protection clause of the Fourteenth Amendment by separating colored people from white people, provided that the facilities were equal. The concept was used again and again, only to be abandoned in the 1950's when the Supreme Court took the position that in education and recreation separate facilities were inherently unequal.

The concept of stream of commerce was developed to get away from the position that interstate commerce was to be thought of in terms of separate articles of shipment and as beginning and ending with the beginning and ending of the transportation of particular items. The Supreme Court found instead that the separate items of shipment could constitute a stream which could be regulated by Congress in spite of the fact that particular items "came to rest" within the area sought to be regulated. In other words, the concept was used to justify broader regulation by Congress than seemed justified when the commerce was atomized into individual units. It lost much of its importance as the Court came to hold that Congress could regulate not only that which was itself interstate commerce but also those things that so affected interstate commerce as to require regulation for the protection of the commerce, whether the regulated items themselves were interstate commerce or not.

The rule of reason was invoked, for the first time officially in 1911, for use in the interpretation of the Sherman Act. The statute outlawed combinations in restraint of interstate trade. It was recognized that any combination might in some degree restrain trade across state lines even though it might not be generally detrimental, and that Congress had not intended to enact an absolute prohibition. The Supreme Court, after debating the issue in a number of cases, virtually read into the statute its "rule of reason" to the effect that the statute prohibited only those combinations "unreasonably" restraining interstate trade. The concept remains in good standing and is taken so much as a matter of course that it seldom requires rearticulation. It has provided analogies for judicial thinking in other fields as well as that of antitrust legislation.

The clear and present danger concept, discussed at length in Chapter III, represented an attempt after the close of World War I to provide a formula for determining how far government could go in limiting First Amendment freedoms in the face of a definite public need. As we have seen, the concept, although it had a wide popular appeal, was never fully accepted by the entire Court. Although it received a high degree of acceptance by the majority of the Court around the late 1930's and early 1940's, it seemed to lose its hold as the Court struggled with the security and loyalty issues of the cold-war period. Its significance as a guide to the judiciary is currently much in doubt.

The concept of the primacy of civil liberties, the final concept on our list, and one also discussed in an earlier chapter, got its formal start in a footnote to a case decided in 1938. It moved into the texts of a number of opinions and gave rise to a great deal of controversy, but the issue involved remains unsettled. That is, there is no agreement on the questions whether civil liberties have a greater immunity to invasion than rights of property, and whether there is something close to a presumption of invalidity attached to legislation and administrative action restricting civil liberties. It is possible to use the concept either to give genuine protection to civil liberties or to stake a claim to righteousness through giving it lip service while permitting invasion of civil liberties in particular instances.

Elaboration on the use of these categories and others similar to them would give us much of the story of American constitutional development. Our purpose here, however, is not to give historical content but to illuminate the aims and methods of the Supreme Court. In its decision of cases the central responsibility of the Court is that of relating a Constitution, in which the terms employed are largely undefined, to an ever-changing social, economic, and political pattern. For many constitutional terms, it is true, and particularly for terms used in restrictive provisions, the Court has some guidance from the long-established definitions of the common law. During the period of its own operations, furthermore, it has the limited guidance of its own precedents. But in the field of constitutional development situations are ever changing, so that precedents satisfactory for the time of their establishment may seem incongruous as guides for later periods. Far more than in the realm of private law the judicial function must be, in the words of Justice Cardozo, "dynamic and creative."

5 So it is that in writing opinions justices strive individually for phraseology that will compact meaning and build a bridge between the written Constitution and the current statement of constitutional law. So it is that, as in the instance of the categories or formulas listed above, groups of justices over decades, or seemingly even permanently, adopt concepts such as that of police power or business affected with a public interest and use them almost as if they were written into the Constitution. Yet if and when these concepts become outmoded, the Court either moves away from them without formal announcement or, as in the instance of the separate but equal formula, directly and flatly rejects them. While particular justices or the Court as a whole for a given period may feel as much bound by their own formulations as if they were direct constitutional commands, succeeding generations of justices will drift away from the concepts in question unless they meet a continuing need.

We are approaching here the difficult and in large measure unanswerable question to what extent the Supreme Court should be bound by its own precedents, thereby ensuring stability in the law and providing guidance for bench and bar and people. As Justice Cardozo made clear, in our quest for certainty we long ago shifted the emphasis from principle to precedents, under the illusion that the latter provided the more stable guide. But we have built up such a mass of precedents that by selective use of them we can prove almost anything—which, in the end, means: practically nothing. In his language, "now at last the precedents have turned upon us and are engulfing and annihilating us—annihilating and engulfing the very devotees that worshiped at their shrine." [26] In this predicament the Court has been torn between the alternatives of going back to principle or shifting with the neorealists to the bare bones of things decided as distinguished from the things said in arriving at decisions.

When the Court itself is in a quandary about its own performance, it is not surprising that laymen should be deeply bewildered and should jump to the oversimplified conclusion that the Court is utterly erratic or is following nothing but individual biases or is yielding to the pressures of the hour, in spite of the protections of the judicial position written into the Constitution to free it as fully as possible from such pressures. Yet close observation indicates that it is a quandary produced by almost insoluble problems rather than by mere political-mindedness—though the latter may not be unimportant—that creates much of our puzzlement. The pattern of argument over the extent of the responsibility of the Court to the desires of the people is well reflected by two quotations from Justice Frankfurter, which at first glance seem to be in conflict. One reads as follows:

> And so, in the end, it is right that the Court should be indifferent to public temper and popular wishes. Mr. Dooley's "the Supreme Court follows th' iliction returns" expressed the wit of cynicism, not the demand of principle. A court which yields to the popular will thereby licenses itself to practice despotism, for there can be no assurance that it will not on another occasion indulge its own will.[27]

Yet with respect to the meaning of due process Justice Frankfurter elsewhere said (see passage quoted on p. 55) that the Court could resort to the "permanent and pervasive feelings of our society," provided those feelings were revealed by "compelling evidence." That evidence must be of the kind "relevant to judgments on our social institutions." [28] But the term relevant is left undefined, and we remain in doubt as to when the Supreme Court may accept guidance from the people in matters of constitutional interpretation. Whether or not he would accept the characterization, it is casting no aspersions on Justice Frankfurter's analysis to say that here, as in so many aspects of life, deep probing eventually takes us close to the realm of the mystical, to a realm where mere intellectualization and logical phrasing fail us, leaving us to feelings and perceptions that make their appearance from we know not where but which nevertheless have for us compelling weight.

Indeed, failing in our efforts to go beyond the range of Justice Frankfurter's analysis and nevertheless finding that his analysis takes us but part of the way in explaining the relation of the Court to the public in deciding constitutional questions, we turn for a helpful literary figure from a jurist to a poet, a "children's poet," as he dealt with relationships in a very different field. It may be that the interrelations between Court and public are aptly suggested by relations between man and woman as portrayed in Longfellow's *Song of Hiawatha,* at the beginning of the section entitled "Hiawatha's Wooing":

> As unto the bow the cord is,
> So unto the man is woman,
> Though she bends him she obeys him,
> Though she draws him, yet she follows,
> Useless each without the other!

Certain it is that between Court and public there is at once a tautness of relation and a give-and-take on the part of each with respect to the other. In some degree each bends the other, and in some degree each obeys.

In carrying this topic to its logical conclusion, furthermore, we have to remember that the Supreme Court not only decides its own cases but also, through the process of decision, provides leadership in constitutional development for lower federal courts and for state courts. For these other tribunals it is a kind of constitutional bellwether. However much they may grumble in private about Supreme Court decisions, they rarely refuse to follow them, and occasional obstreperous refusal to follow, as in the instance of segregation in schools, delays only temporarily the working out of the policy set by the Supreme Court. Since it determines the pattern of constitutional decisions in the other courts, the Supreme Court in effect determines it for the other branches of government as well. In other words, the Supreme Court spearheads the process of constitutional unfolding for all branches and agencies of government and for all the people.

Oligarchic though the Court is in channeling and restricting the exercise of power, it cannot completely ignore either the need for consistency with the past and with past decisions or an almost implacable drift in public sentiment as to what constitutional limitations and prerogatives ought to be. The "quest for certainty," the need for certainty on the part of all of us, is too great to permit wholesale abandonment of past lines of decision. Yet as Justice Holmes well said some sixty years ago, "We do not realize how large a part of our law is open to reconsideration upon a slight change in the habit of the public mind. No concrete proposition is self-evident, no matter how ready we may be to accept it. . . ." [29] Relevant also are the implications of his assertion that "The foundation of jurisdiction is physical power." [30] The Supreme Court has, strictly within itself, only the physical power of nine men well beyond their prime. It is a powerful body—the most powerful court in the world—because it has back of it the power of the political branches of the government, which in turn have power only because they have the support and have at their call the resources of the American people.

The Supreme Court is able to lead in constitutional development, then, only by virtue of the fact that its leadership is of such a character that the people and their representatives are willing to follow. To put the matter more simply, the Supreme Court succeeds in leading largely to the extent of its skill not merely as a leader but as a follower. Since the medium of its leadership is the law, or the decision of cases in terms of law, we can go further and say that the effectiveness of the Court's leadership is measured by its ability to articulate deep convictions of need and deep patterns of desire on the part of the people in such a way that the people, who might not have been able themselves to be similarly articulate, will recognize the judicial statement as essentially their own. The Court must sense the synthesis of desire for both continuity and change and make the desired synthesis the expressed pattern of each decision.

6 In understanding the work of the Court we must remember, furthermore, that notwithstanding the disillusionment that comes with the convictions of individuals and groups that particular decisions are wrong, and notwithstanding the criticism of justices one of another in the decision of cases, the people tend ordinarily to think of the Court as something much more than an aggregate of nine statesmen of high rectitude and learning in the law. They think of it as a court, as a tribunal, as an organic whole. For constitutional leadership they look not to an aggregation of nine individual leaders but to an organic unit of one tribunal, one court. To the extent of its inability to integrate into its decisions and into opinions of the Court the best that individual justices have to offer, the Court fails the people and fails in fulfillment of its proper function of leadership.

We do not of course condemn the Supreme Court for failing to live up completely to its ideal, any more than we would so condemn any other institution. Amid the storm-center pressures that converge on the Court it is not to be expected that nine men of mature years, diversely trained and with diverse approaches to the law, should in all instances be able to yield their best to a synthesis in an opinion of the Court. But the ideal is there as a goal to strive toward.[31] It is of course true that men not adversely affected take delight in brilliant individual statements by such justices as Holmes, Brandeis, Cardozo, Frankfurter, Black, and Douglas. Furthermore, if the opinion of the Court proves a work of poor craftsmanship, men learned in the techniques of the law take delight in concurring opinions that set matters right as to technique, in spite of the discredit done to the opinion of the Court. And there are undoubtedly times when justices with a sense of deep personal integrity must divorce themselves from the unsatisfactory statements prepared by their brethren or perhaps dissent altogether. But the fact remains that, to the extent of the inability of justices to agree on decisions and on statements of the law, the Court as a whole has failed to complete the performance of its ideal function.

The opinion of the Court, then, is a statement in terms of law of the "permanent and pervasive feelings of our society" that Justice Frankfurter talks about. It is a microcosmic statement of that which exists unclearly stated in the macrocosm, but the microcosm is the Court, and not the individual justice. Indeed, the very existence of the Court, of nine men merged in one tribunal, stands as an article of faith in the existence of a society that is something more than an atomized structure, that functions as a kind of organic whole and yields to guidance from some inner-directed body of constitutional idealism. The function of the Court is to make articulate that body of idealism and demonstrate the capacity for the merging of the each in the all, to the extent of the performance of nine men selected for that purpose, of nine men out of the millions who make up our total population.

With the above as a statement of the ideal goal of judicial endeavor, how shall we appraise the work of the Supreme Court since the critical days of the New Deal? That work must be appraised in terms of its time setting. It is to be remembered that prior to the transition which began in 1937 the Court had been dominated by men whose economic thinking was conservative and that their position had had the support of dominant interests in the country. At the same time, a minority faction consisting of Justices Holmes, Brandeis, and Stone, with Justice Cardozo replacing Justice Holmes in 1932, had been building largely through dissenting opinions a body of doctrine that is generally called liberal, with a growing support among the people. Although dislike of extreme measures and undisciplined procedure brought the entire Court together in opposition to certain New Deal measures, the breach was not healed, and the so-called liberal justices seemed more comfortable when they were again on opposite sides from at least the four ultraconservatives on the Court. New Deal sentiment aligned itself behind the liberal justices as if the New Deal program had had their full support, so that the liberals, probably with mixed feelings, found themselves the leaders of the diverse elements that were aligning themselves against economic conservatism and on the side of paternalistic programs and maximum protection for civil liberties. New justices appointed to the Court, beginning with the appointment of Justice Black in 1937, were themselves New Dealers, and they regarded themselves as the legitimate successors of the liberal minority group that they gradually replaced, as they replaced also the ultraconservatives. They assumed that they had a mandate to divert the trend of decisions away from economic conservatism and to clear judicial obstructions from the path of the government as it sought to promote economic welfare and to make impossible tragedies such as that represented by the great depression. With elements of idealism and ruthlessness they went about their task, with the zeal but often without the courtesy and personal objectivity and self-restraint hitherto displayed by the liberal minority.

We must not forget, it is true, that the shift in the trend of interpretation began even before the appointment of the first of the Roosevelt justices. Whatever the weight of impact of the attempt to pack the Court during the early months of 1937, it was during that period that the Court shifted its ground to permit governmental regulation of minimum wages,[32] upheld the National Labor Relations Act as to regulation of labor in production affecting interstate commerce,[33] and also upheld use of the taxing and spending power to support a social security program.[34] Already, in the language of the liberals, the Court was getting "back to the Constitution." It is not here contended that the Court was merely "following the election returns." The new trend was in harmony with the trend of elections, but it might more appropriately be said, in defending the Court against the charge of merely political behavior, that both the elections and the Courts were responding to deep and abiding sentiments in the body politic that had not hitherto won recognition either by the political or by the judicial branches of the government.

As the Roosevelt justices achieved a majority on the Court, precedents continued to fall until the way had been cleared for a program of economic liberalism and then for the war program. Yet the justices who were in their own minds headed "back to the Constitution," while convinced that they knew the direction, had unprecedented difficulty in identifying the contours of what they were going back to. Instead of moving into agreement now that economic conservatism had been defeated, they rode off in all directions in their search, and turned upon one another with unprecedented savagery even in published opinions.[35] So great was the diversity of approach that in important cases it was at times impossible to get a majority to agree on an opinion of the Court, and when opinions of the Court were written they were often so hedged about by concurring and dissenting opinions that neither bench nor bar nor people could find guidance in them. If it could not be said, in scriptural language, that much learning had made the justices mad, something had at least made them very verbose and apparently very angry.

We are still much too close to the work of the Court from 1935 to 1955 to appraise it with confidence. We may suggest that the successors to Justices Holmes and Brandeis were zealots without the self-discipline of their masters,[36] that they were professional soldiers who knew not how to stop fighting and to make peace after their war was won, but had to go on fighting because they did not know how to do anything else. But the explanation probably goes much deeper. The trend away from economic conservatism involved tremendous and often conflicting pressures that were inevitably felt by the justices, for all the aloofness of their positions. Courts could no longer be insensitive to those pressures of major war—

with which, indeed, they actually merged. It is probable that any Supreme Court, however constituted, would have displayed great diversity of opinion in the face of such pressures.

For another explanation we may go back to Roscoe Pound's assertion in 1914 that we had been a law-ridden people. Already, Pound thought, that characteristic had changed. He thought it was "not without much reason" that we had come to be called "a lawless people." [37] Certain it is that during the twentieth century, with the shift of emphasis to public administration, we have abandoned the tendency to make every question a legal question in the sense of a question to be decided by a court. The trend toward legal realism has in great part dispelled the halo that dwelt around the law and the judiciary. It is not surprising that, as the judiciary misconceived its function and became the spokesman for dominant economic interests rather than for the abiding sentiments of all the people, the critics of the courts, and even members of the Supreme Court, should join in the attack on the once-hallowed institution.

It is no doubt true that purging attacks on the judiciary, both from without and from within, have eliminated much obsolete material. Yet as the Supreme Court majority continued the attacks begun by the earlier minority, and found itself eventually attacking itself and not some external enemy, it reached a stage where it was without an adequate defender. If the Court is to pursue an ideal, the members of the Court must believe in the ideal and in the Court itself. It is a matter for deep concern when a justice can accept the fact, as did Justice Jackson shortly before his death, that "the Court functions less as one deliberative body than as nine." [38] It is likewise a matter for deep concern when with the frequency of recent years individual justices deem the work of the Court as a whole so inadequate as to obligate them to enshroud opinions of the Court with diverse individual opinions.

Yet, to repeat, the fault may not lie merely, or even primarily, with the members of the Court, but with the opportunism of our times, with a lack of concern about and commitment to what Walter Lippmann has called the public philosophy.[39] If we as a people lose sight of our "public philosophy," if we cease our groping for the things that abide, we cannot expect our judges indefinitely to pursue the search for what we have ceased to believe in or to account it of sufficient worth to justify the pursuit. With respect to our political philosophy, there can be no leadership unless there are people willing to be led; there can be no effective propagation of constitutional belief unless there are people who are willing to believe, who indeed do believe already and but await the articulation that leaders provide. It may well be, therefore, as in Shakespeare's portrayal of Cassius and Brutus long ago, that the fault lies not primarily in the Supreme Court, or even in our stars, but in ourselves, if we have at times wallowed in conditions approaching judicial chaos rather than legal order.

7 In the light of the things said here, what can we predict about Supreme Court performance in the years lying just ahead? There are too many variables in the situation to permit confident prediction in any direction. What the Court does will depend to a great extent on what the people do and on what they want. We may see a return to ideals or to a search for ideals that will provide more guidance than resort to the expediencies of the moment or reliance on sheer physical or political power. If the people come to demonstrate an idealism and a concern with principle such as were characteristic of the time of the adoption of the Constitution, the judiciary may be expected, even if belatedly, to echo that idealism in the interpretation of law. If we become more and more disillusioned with principle and more and more convinced that nothing counts but power, whether physical or political or both, then we may expect the judiciary, again perhaps belatedly but nevertheless inevitably, to reflect the dominant sentiment, a sentiment that will stand in the way

of the building of a body of law with a stable ethical core and with manifestations in all walks of life. In other words, we are likely to get from our judiciary pretty much what we ask for—which may be about the same as saying that we shall get what we deserve.

But the future will inevitably be shaped in part by factors beyond our control. Whatever our own performances, the behavior of powerful Communist nations may keep us in the position of an armed camp, in a state of cold war if not in actual military conflict, and war devastating beyond all possibility of imagination could well be in the picture. As we have seen, the judiciary in time of war is not disposed to interfere basically with the conduct of the military, and even with the political, branches of government, and neither the government nor the people invite judicial interference when the life of the nation is at stake. Under such circumstances the judiciary is left with the alternatives of staying out of the picture or of giving speedy judicial approval and rationalization to whatever action the government sees fit to take. Such conditions are anything but ideal for the orderly development of law, for the normal functioning of the judiciary.

It is possible, on the other hand, that the drift will be in the other direction. The world may gradually cease to be mesmerized by the Communist nations, and the hard core within those nations may become so softened as to permit them to live peaceably in the "One World" that was dimly envisaged at the time of the establishment of the United Nations. Restoration of world order and the resumption of efforts to build a body of world law may create an appropriate atmosphere for emphasis on legality within our own borders. It may bring on the part of our own judiciary a reinvigorated search for principles to be used in constitutional unfolding. It could bring a new regime of liberty under law, with the judiciary playing a prominent part in charting legal development. But these possibilities, to repeat, are to be measured not alone by what we the American people choose to do at home or by our aims and our skill in negotiating abroad: they depend in large part on what other peoples do, and we shall have to adjust to forces partly beyond our own control.

Speaking in terms strictly of the Supreme Court, much will depend on the selection of personnel as incumbent members retire. We have already left behind the period when new justices were sure to be selected from crusading members of the New Deal—if for no other reason than that the major aspects of the New Deal are now so much part of our day-to-day living that they are no longer thought of in terms of a crusade. The four most recent appointees, indeed, including the present Chief Justice, reflect an atmosphere vastly different from that created by their immediate predecessors, who revealed a sense of mission with respect to the success of particular governmental programs, and their ultraconservative predecessors of an earlier period, who showed a similar sense of mission in seeing to it that liberal programs were curbed by judicially erected barriers. Continued careful choice of personnel can give us a poise and objectivity that has not been witnessed in the Court as a whole for many years.

Some seemingly minor factors are not without influence. Chief Justice Taft was largely instrumental in having the Court housed in a building of its own, with offices for the justices and their staffs and with a central library available for all their needs. While his concern was partly with demonstrating the equality of the judiciary with the other two branches of the government, each of which had always had its own central building, his concern was probably broader than that. He may well have envisaged the decades of the Marshall period and part of the Taney period when for the brief term of the Court all the justices lived in one hotel, ate their meals together, and carried on congenial fraternal life as a part of their judicial performance. For many intervening decades justices not only had their homes in Washington but also had their offices in their homes, so that they met as a body only on official occasions. A Supreme Court building bore the promise of bringing them back together again for their official activities.

But as illustrated by Justice Jackson's statement, quoted above, that "the Court functions less as one deliberative body than as nine," Taft's hopes on this point were not fulfilled. In their palatial offices the justices continued to go their own ways. Furthermore, expansion of facilities and increased appropriations made possible the increase of staff services, which were partly centralized for the Court as a whole but partly decentralized in the clerks and secretaries of individual justices. The latter tended to develop into "rooting sections" for their particular employers, with increased tendency to fragmentize the Court. Whereas justices generations ago had composed their differences in private and had kept few or no records to show where they had yielded to pressure from majorities, the operations of present justices are visible to, are participated in by, staffs who constitute a kind of inner pressure group on the Court and who, in degrees varying with the personalities involved, hold out for disputed positions instead of seeking creative compromise. When law clerks are permitted, as they were by Justice Stone, "to use footnotes as trial balloons for meritorious ideas," [40] or when, as the grapevine has it, other justices use or have used clerks to write rough drafts of their opinions, weight is added to the desire to maintain the position of individual justices and to oppose compromise. It would seem, indeed, that Justice Stone's secretary as well as his law clerk operated as a goad to individual rather than group expression. On one occasion when Chief Justice Hughes got high praise for an opinion of the Court to which Stone had contributed anonymously, his secretary is reported to have recorded: "I think H.F.S. was cured and will write his dissents and concurrences in the future, for all his hesitation to do so." [41]

The use of clerks by the justices follows somewhat the pattern of staff development in the executive branch of the government, where the accumulation and organization of facts are done by staff as a matter of course and where documents, even the official opinions of members of quasi-judicial agencies, are drafted and presented to top officials for their signature. The use of staff by members of the Supreme Court has gone by no means so far, but when justices are appointed from administrative positions in which staff was so employed, it is not surprising that the practice tends to carry over. The use of law clerks is sufficiently extensive, however, to lead to the humorous or rueful suggestion that Senate confirmation of appointment of law clerks might become more important than confirmation of the justices. Justice Jackson expressed what still seems to be the dominant sentiment about the matter when he said, "I do not think judging can be a staff job, and I deplore whatever tendency there may be in the courts to make it such." [42]

If judicial staffs can be disruptive factors and can obstruct compromises necessary to the merging of multiple opinions in an opinion of the Court, so also can the outside associates and correspondents of the justices, including former secretaries with whom some justices continue to discuss the work of the Court. Alpheus Mason's impressive biography of Justice Stone shows that Stone conducted a monumental correspondence of a kind that must have had much to do with the development of his thinking as a judge. If other justices are in varying degrees more reticent about their official performance, they nevertheless have wide associations that are to be taken into account in any appraisal of their development. While law school professors and former clerks and Washington neighbors employed in the legislative and executive branches may not have an insidious influence comparable to that of the buccaneers of big business and their lawyers, who were said to be too much in the company of the justices many decades ago, their thinking probably is not without influence on the work of the Court.

All this is not to suggest that justices ought to be housed in a monastery or that the selection of their friends—and perhaps also of their wives—ought to be subject to confirmation by the Senate. It is merely to suggest the multiple difficulties of maintaining a tribunal that is intellectually alive and creative and that can nevertheless operate as a unit rather than as an aggregation of nine men, each with his clerical, secretarial, and popular following, which he is under social pressure in some measure to satisfy by evidence that he is making himself felt and is not merely the instrument of a group of other justices.

There are other problems of which we shall mention only one, and leave that one largely undiscussed. It is the problem of nine men who have inevitably led active lives climbing from position to position until they finally reach the Supreme Court. Now, except for the occasional individual who hopes to use his judicial office as a steppingstone to the presidency—a hope that has never been fulfilled—there is no place else to go. A Supreme Court justice has arrived. He has to adjust his lifelong habit of climbing to the fact that his energies from now on are to be expended right where he is. Some justices in earlier years have responded by gradually sinking into a kind of somnolence after the novelty of judicial performance had worn off. Others, more admirably but nevertheless regrettably, unable either to go to sleep or to work efficiently with judicial anonymity, have plunged into a search for continuing uniqueness by pursuing individually chosen goals in the decision of cases, by writing concurring or dissenting opinions on fascinating tangents and marring thereby their own value as anonymous contributors to constitutional synthesis. Perhaps what these men need is a renewed sense of the law developed by the Court as worthy of deep devotion, as something worthy of the full commitment of the judge, as something in which he can merge his identity with a sense of high achievement rather than with a sense of defeat and annihilation.

However that may be, the Supreme Court in its modern role is a fascinating subject for observation. It operates at the storm center of our national life, it manifests the loftiness of our constitutional ideals, it touches us to the quick at the focal points of our basic drives as economic, racial, political, and military groups and as a democracy, and it displays the diversity of the human menagerie in which all of us play a part. Its close observers commend it to all who would develop a deeper understanding of man in his struggle toward higher things.

Notes

CHAPTER I

1. Robert H. Jackson, *The Struggle for Judicial Supremacy* (1941), p. xv.
2. *Ibid.*, p. xiv.
3. Benjamin N. Cardozo, *The Paradoxes of Legal Science* (1928), p. 2.
4. United States v. Butler, 297 U.S. 1, 87 (1936).
5. *Ibid.*, p. 78.
6. West Coast Hotel Co. v. Parrish, 300 U.S. 379, 402 (1937).
7. Mississippi v. Johnson, 4 Wallace 475, 500-501 (1867).
8. Marbury v. Madison, 1 Cranch 137, 177 (1803).
9. Charles Warren, *The Supreme Court in United States History* (1928 printing), Vol. I, p. 759.
10. Sir William Blackstone, *Commentaries on the Laws of England* (1769), Vol. I, p. 267.
11. See Edward S. Corwin, *The "Higher Law" Background of American Constitutional Law* (reprinted, 1955), pp. 55-56.
12. Jonathan Elliot, *The Debates in the Several Conventions on the Adoption of the Federal Constitution* (1861), Vol. III, p. 564.
13. *The Correspondence and Public Papers of John Jay* (1893), Vol. IV, p. 285.
14. Allison Dunham and Philip B. Kurland (eds.), *Mr. Justice* (1956), p. 22.
15. Donald G. Morgan, *Justice William Johnson, The First Dissenter* (1954), p. 182.
16. William Wirt, *Letters of the British Spy* (5th ed., 1813), pp. 95-96.
17. *Ibid.*, pp. 97-98.
18. Marbury v. Madison, 1 Cranch 137, 177 (1803).
19. Fletcher v. Peck, 6 Cranch 87 (1810). For discussion, see Benjamin F. Wright, *The Contract Clause of the Constitution* (1938), chaps. i and ii.
20. Dartmouth College v. Woodward, 4 Wheaton 518 (1819).
21. 12 Wheaton 213 (1827).
22. See Martin v. Hunter's Lessee, 1 Wheaton 304 (1816), and Cohens v. Virginia, 6 Wheaton 264 (1821).

23. McCulloch v. Maryland, 4 Wheaton 316, 431 (1819).
24. Gibbons v. Ogden, 9 Wheaton 1 (1824).
25. Craig v. Missouri, 4 Peters 410 (1830).
26. Charles River Bridge v. Warren Bridge, 11 Peters 420, 547 (1837).
27. *Ibid.*, p. 548.
28. *Ibid.*, p. 584.
29. Briscoe v. Bank of the Commonwealth of Kentucky, 11 Peters 257, 327 (1837).
30. *Ibid.*, p. 350.
31. New York v. Miln, 11 Peters 102, 161 (1837).
32. Carl Brent Swisher, *Roger B. Taney* (1935), p. 403.
33. "The Supreme Court of the United States," *United States Magazine and Democratic Review,* Vol. I (June, 1840), pp. 503-504.
34. See Swisher, *op. cit.*, chap. xxvii.
35. See especially Mississippi v. Johnson, 4 Wallace 475 (1867), and Georgia v. Stanton, 6 Wallace 50 (1867).
36. See *Ex parte* McCardle, 6 Wallace 318 (1868), 7 Wallace 506 (1869).
37. *Ex parte* Milligan, 4 Wallace 2 (1866). For discussion, see Chapter IV.
38. Texas v. White, 7 Wallace 700 (1869).
39. Hepburn v. Griswold, 8 Wallace 603 (1870).
40. Legal Tender Cases (Knox v. Lee and Parker v. Davis), 12 Wallace 457 (1871).
41. Both quotations are taken from Charles Fairman, *Mr. Justice Miller and the Supreme Court* (1939), p. 140.
42. See, for example, United States v. Cruikshank, 92 U.S. 542 (1876), United States v. Reese, 92 U.S. 214 (1876), and Civil Rights Cases, 109 U.S. 3 (1883).
43. 16 Wallace 36 (1873).
44. *Ibid.*, p. 89.
45. *Ibid.*, p. 93.
46. *Ibid.*, p. 95.
47. *Ibid.*, p. 97.
48. *Ibid.*, p. 105.
49. *Ibid.*, p. 122.
50. *Ibid.*, p. 129.
51. Munn v. Illinois, 94 U.S. 113, 134 (1877).
52. *Ibid.*, p. 152.
53. Stone v. Farmers' Loan and Trust Co., 116 U.S. 307, 331 (1886).
54. Lochner v. New York, 198 U.S. 45, 75 (1905).
55. *Ibid.*, p. 75.
56. Muller v. Oregon, 208 U.S. 412 (1908).
57. Bunting v. Oregon, 243 U.S. 426 (1917).
58. Adkins v. Children's Hospital, 261 U.S. 525 (1923).
59. Nebbia v. New York, 291 U.S. 502 (1934).
60. 157 U.S. 429, 158 U.S. 601.

61. 157 U.S. 607.
62. Knowlton v. Moore, 178 U.S. 41 (1900).
63. Flint v. Stone Tracy Co., 240 U.S. 1 (1911).
64. For discussion, see Carl Brent Swisher, *American Constitutional Development* (2d ed., 1954), pp. 475 ff.
65. See, for example, Selective Draft Law Cases (Arver v. United States), 245 U.S. 366 (1918), and United States v. Curtiss-Wright Export Corporation, 299 U.S. 304 (1936).
66. Adair v. United States, 208 U.S. 161 (1908).
67. Texas and New Orleans Railroad Co. v. Brotherhood of Railway and Steamship Clerks, 281 U.S. 548 (1930).
68. Hoke v. United States, 227 U.S. 308, 322 (1913).
69. Hammer v. Dagenhart, 247 U.S. 251 (1918).
70. See Schechter Poultry Corp. v. United States, 295 U.S. 495 (1935), and Carter v. Carter Coal Co., 298 U.S. 238 (1936).
71. See, for example, United States v. Darby, 312 U.S. 100 (1941).
72. Appalachian Coals Co. v. United States, 288 U.S. 344, 359-360 (1932).
73. United States v. E. C. Knight Co., 156 U.S. 1 (1895).
74. See, for example, Standard Oil Co. v. United States, 221 U.S. 1 (1911), and the statement there of the so-called "rule of reason."
75. See McGrain v. Daugherty, 273 U.S. 135 (1927), Sinclair v. United States, 279 U.S. 263 (1929), and Barry v. United States *ex rel.* Cunningham, 279 U.S. 597 (1929).
76. See *Ex parte* Grossman, 267 U.S. 87 (1925), and Biddle v. Perovich, 274 U.S. 480 (1927).
77. 272 U.S. 52 (1926).
78. Humphrey's Executor (Rathbun) v. United States, 295 U.S. 602 (1935).
79. The author has discussed this subject at length in his *American Constitutional Development* (2d ed., 1954), chap. xxxvi.
80. Quoted above, p. 5.
81. Appalachian Coals Co. v. United States, 288 U.S. 344, 359-360 (1932).

CHAPTER II

1. Marbury v. Madison, 1 Cranch 137, 177 (1803).
2. *Ibid.*, p. 180.
3. Oliver Wendell Holmes, *Collected Legal Papers* (1920), p. 292.

4. *Ex parte* Garland, 4 Wallace 33 (1867).
5. See pp. 12-15.
6. Barron v. Baltimore, 7 Peters 243 (1833).
7. Den *ex dem.* Murray v. Hoboken Land and Improvement Co., 18 Howard 272, 276 (1856).
8. *Ibid.*, p. 277.
9. *Ibid.*, p. 276.
10. 110 U.S. 516 (1884).
11. *Ibid.*, p. 537.
12. 302 U.S. 319.
13. *Ibid.*, pp. 324-325.
14. *Ibid.*, p. 325, quoting from Snyder v. Massachusetts, 291 U.S. 97, 105 (1934).
15. *The Works of John Adams*, Vol. VI (1851), pp. 8-9. The Field citation is in a dissenting opinion, Central Pacific Co. v. Gallatin, 99 U.S. 727, 767 (1879).
16. Edward S. Corwin, *Liberty Against Government* (1948), p. 138; see also Charles G. Haines, *The Revival of Natural Law Concepts* (1930).
17. See especially Allgeyer v. Louisiana, 165 U.S. 578 (1897), and Lochner v. New York, 198 U.S. 45 (1905).
18. Nebbia v. New York, 291 U.S. 502 (1934).
19. 169 U.S. 466.
20. Federal Power Commission v. Natural Gas Pipeline Co., 315 U.S. 575, 586 (1942).
21. Federal Power Commission v. Hope Natural Gas Co., 320 U.S. 584, 601 (1944).
22. Truax v. Corrigan, 257 U.S. 312, 344 (1921).
23. See Felix Frankfurter, *Mr. Justice Holmes and the Supreme Court* (1938), pp. 50-51.
24. Whitney v. California, 274 U.S. 357, 374 (1927).
25. Prudential Insurance Co. v. Cheek, 259 U.S. 530, 543 (1922).
26. Gitlow v. New York, 268 U.S. 652, 666 (1925).
27. Palko v. Connecticut, 302 U.S. 319, 327 (1937). For earlier contributing cases see Charles Warren, "The New Liberty Under the Fourteenth Amendment," *Harvard Law Review*, Vol. XXXIX, p. 431.
28. United States v. Carolene Products Co., 304 U.S. 144, 152-154, note 4 (1938).
29. Alpheus T. Mason, *Harlan Fiske Stone: Pillar of the Law* (1956), p. 513.
30. United States v. Butler, 297 U.S. 1, 78, 79 (1936).
31. West Virginia State Board of Education v. Barnette, 319 U.S. 624, 641 (1943).
32. *Ibid.*, p. 639.
33. *Ibid.*, p. 648.
34. Thomas v. Collins, 323 U.S. 516, 530 (1945). See the language of Justice Douglas dissenting in Black v. Cut-

ter Laboratories, 351 U.S. 292, 300 (1956).

35. For summary, see Kovacs v. Cooper, 336 U.S. 77, 90-96 (1949).
36. See, for example, Kovacs v. Cooper, 336 U.S. 87-89 (1949).
37. *Ibid.*, p. 90.
38. Dennis v. United States, 341 U.S. 491, 527 (1951).
39. Thomas v. Collins, 323 U.S. 516 (1945).
40. 332 U.S. 46.
41. 211 U.S. 78.
42. See pp. 40-41.
43. Adamson v. California, 332 U.S. 46, 89 (1947).
44. *Ibid.*, p. 89.
45. *Ibid.*, p. 75.
46. *Ibid.*, p. 59.
47. *Ibid.*, pp. 64-65.
48. *Ibid.*, p. 65.
49. *Ibid.*, pp. 67-68.
50. *Ibid.*, p. 124.
51. See Wolf v. Colorado, 338 U.S. 25 (1949).
52. For a suggestion of uncertainty in Chief Justice Warren's position, see Regan v. New York, 349 U.S. 58, 65-66 (1955).
53. Haley v. Ohio, 332 U.S. 596-602 (1948).
54. *Ibid.*, p. 603.
55. *Ibid.*, p. 605.
56. Solesbee v. Balkcom, 339 U.S. 9, 16 (1950).
57. Wolf v. Colorado, 338 U.S. 25, 26 (1949).
58. Rochin v. California, 342 U.S. 165, 172 (1952).
59. Irvine v. California, 347 U.S. 128, 146 (1954).
60. *Ibid.*, p. 144.
61. *Ibid.*, p. 138.
62. Williamson v. Lee Optical of Oklahoma, 348 U.S. 483, 488 (1955).
63. Yick Wo v. Hopkins, 118 U.S. 356-369 (1886).
64. Goesaert v. Cleary, 335 U.S. 464 (1948).
65. *Ibid.*, p. 466.
66. Semler v. Oregon State Dental Examiners, 294 U.S. 608 (1935).
67. Railway Express Agency v. New York, 336 U.S. 106 (1949).
68. Tigner v. Texas, 310 U.S. 141 (1940).
69. Williamson v. Lee Optical of Oklahoma, 348 U.S. 483 (1955).
70. 331 U.S. 145.
71. 334 U.S. 699.
72. 339 U.S. 56.
73. Olmstead v. United States, 277 U.S. 438 (1928).
74. Goldman v. United States, 316 U.S. 129 (1942).
75. On Lee v. United States, 343 U.S. 747, 752 (1952).
76. *Ibid.*, p. 767.

CHAPTER III

1. Cramer v. United States, 325 U.S. 1, 26 (1945).
2. See, for example, Willard Hurst, "Treason in the United States," *Harvard Law Review,* Vol. LVIII, pp. 226-272, 395-444, 806-846.
3. See Rosenberg v. United States, 346 U.S. 273 (1953).
4. *Ex parte* Bollman, 4 Cranch 75 (1807).
5. Charles Page Smith, *James Wilson: Founding Father* (1956), pp. 123, 246.
6. See United States v. Burr, 25 Federal Cases 2, No. 14, 692a (1807).
7. See Carl Brent Swisher, *Stephen J. Field: Craftsman of the Law* (1930), pp. 130-132.
8. See Carl Brent Swisher, *Roger B. Taney* (1935), chap. xxvi.
9. *Ex parte Quirin,* 317 U.S. 1 (1942).
10. 325 U.S. 1 (1945).
11. *Ibid.,* pp. 48-49.
12. Hurst, *op. cit.,* p. 806.
13. Haupt v. United States, 330 U.S. 631, 642 (1947).
14. *Ibid.,* p. 642.
15. Kawakita v. United States, 343 U.S. 717, 735 (1952).
16. Hurst, *op. cit.,* p. 806.
17. 1 Stat. 597,
18. Abrams v. United States, 250 U.S. 616, 630 (1919).
19. Schenck v. United States, 249 U.S. 47, 52 (1919).
20. *Ibid.,* p. 52.
21. Samuel J. Konefsky, *The Legacy of Holmes and Brandeis* (1956), p. 192.
22. *Ibid.,* p. 218.
23. *Ibid.,* p. 202.
24. Schaefer v. United States, 251 U.S. 466, 482 (1920).
25. Alexander Meiklejohn, *Free Speech and Its Relation to Self-Government* (1948), p. 29.
26. Zachariah Chafee, Jr., *Free Speech in the United States* (1941), p. 82.
27. Dennis v. United States, 341 U.S. 494, 567, note 9 (1951).
28. West Virginia State Board of Education v. Barnette, 319 U.S. 624, 663 (1943).
29. Pennekamp v. Florida, 328 U.S. 331, 353 (1946).
30. See Gitlow v. New York, 268 U.S. 652 (1925).
31. Bridges v. California, 314 U.S. 252, 263 (1941).
32. Pennekamp v. Florida, 328 U.S. 331, 353 (1946).
33. American Communications Association v. Douds, 339 U.S. 382, 397 (1950).
34. Dennis v. United States, 341 U.S. 494, 508 (1951).

35. *Ibid.*, pp. 539-540.
36. *Ibid.*, p. 543.
37. *Ibid.*, p. 544.
38. *Ibid.*, p. 568.
39. *Ibid.*, p. 580.
40. *Ibid.*, p. 581.
41. *Ibid.*, p. 589.
42. See Robert Goodloe Harper in *Annals of Congress,* 5th Cong., 2d Sess., 1567-1568. See Carl Brent Swisher, *American Constitutional Development* (2d ed., 1954), pp. 89-91.
43. Mahler v. Eby, 264 U.S. 32, 39 (1924). For original statement of the full power to deport, see Fong Yue Ting v. United States, 149 U.S. 698 (1893).
44. United States *ex rel.* Knauff v. Shaughnessy, 338 U.S. 537, 551-552 (1950).
45. Ludecke v. Watkins, 335 U.S. 160, 183 (1948).
46. *Ibid.*, p. 187.
47. Bridges v. Wixon, 326 U.S. 135, 157 (1945). For a summary of the controversy, see Swisher, *American Constitutional Development*, pp. 1013-1014.
48. Kessler v. Strecker, 307 U.S. 22 (1939).
49. 342 U.S. 580.
50. *Ibid.*, p. 601.
51. Galvan v. Press, 347 U.S. 522, 530-531 (1954).
52. *Ibid.*, p. 534.
53. See, for example, Truax v. Raich, 239 U.S. 33 (1915).
54. Schneiderman v. United States, 320 U.S. 118, 167 (1943). See also Baumgartner v. United States, 322 U.S. 665 (1944).
55. Hirabayashi v. United States, 320 U.S. 81, 100 (1943).
56. Korematsu v. United States, 323 U.S. 214 (1944).
57. *Ex parte* Endo, 323 U.S. 283 (1944).
58. For discussion of the program, see Morton Grodzins, *Americans Betrayed* (1949), Jacobus Ten Broeck *et al., Japanese-American Evacuation and Resettlement* (1944), and Alpheus T. Mason, *Harlan Fiske Stone: Pillar of Society* (1956), chap. xl. For discussion of the use of the military in this situation, see Chapter IV.
59. 314 U.S. 123.
60. Joint Anti-Fascist Refugee Committee v. McGrath, 104 F. Supp. 567, 569-570 (1952).
61. Joint Anti-Fascist Refugee Committee v. McGranery, 345 U.S. 911 (1953).
62. Bailey v. Richardson, 182 F. 2d 46 (1950).
63. Bailey v. Richardson, 341 U.S. 918 (1951).
64. 341 U.S. 179.
65. *Ibid.*, p. 180.
66. *Ibid.*

67. Peters v. Hobby, 349 U.S. 331 (1955).
68. *Ibid.*, pp. 351-352.

Although the controversy over the use of "faceless informers" as a basis of administrative action against government employees has not been settled, the Supreme Court in June, 1957, made an indirect approach to it in a criminal case involving prosecution for perjury of a man accused of falsely swearing that he had not been a member of the Communist party on a specified date. Witnesses against the defendant included party members who secretly were paid informers of the Federal Bureau of Investigation. In order to impeach the testimony of these witnesses, one of whom was himself eventually convicted of perjury in another case, the defendant sought the privilege of inspecting the relevant reports that they had made to the F.B.I. The trial judge denied the request but the Supreme Court reversed the decision, holding that the government must choose between disclosing the reports and giving up prosecution on the basis of the testimony of these witnesses. It was noted that one of them had said, "I don't recall what I put in my reports two or three years ago, written or oral, I don't know what they were." The Supreme Court, through Justice Brennan, stated: "Every experienced trial judge and trial lawyer knows the value for impeaching purposes of statements of the witness recording the events before time dulls treacherous memory. Flat contradiction between the witness's testimony and the version of the events given in his reports is not the only test of inconsistency. The omission from the reports of facts related at the trial, or a contrast in emphasis upon the same facts, even a different order of treatment, are also relevant to the cross-examining process of testing the credibility of a witness's trial testimony." Jencks v. United States, 1 L. Ed. 2d 1103, 1111 (1957).

69. Garner v. Board of Public Works, 341 U.S. 716 (1951).
70. Adler v. Board of Education, 342 U.S. 485 (1952).
71. Wieman v. Updegraff, 344 U.S. 183 (1952).
72. Slochower v. Board of Higher Education, 350 U.S. 551 (1956).
73. On this point see Ullman v. United States, 350 U.S. 422 (1956). For discussion, see Erwin N. Griswold, *The Fifth Amendment Today*

(1955), and Edward A. Shils, *The Torment of Secrecy* (1956).

74. Pennsylvania v. Nelson, 350 U.S. 497 (1956).

75. See Communist Party v. Subversive Activities Control Board, 351 U.S. 115 (1956), and Mesarosh v. United States, 1 L. Ed. 2d, 1 (1956). In a series of cases decided in June, 1957, the Supreme Court in various ways limited government procedures in dealing with persons accused of subversive or "un-American" conduct. In Jencks v. United States, 1 L. Ed. 2d, 1103 (1957), it held that defendants were entitled to access to F.B.I. reports made to the government about the defendants, for the purpose of challenging the authenticity of the testimony. In Yates v. United States, 1 L. Ed. 2d, 1356 (1957), it restricted the application of the Smith Act in connection with the trial of leaders of the Communist party. In Watkins v. United States, 1 L. Ed. 2d, 1273 (1957), it limited the power of congressional investigations to range without restriction and without relation to legislative intent in attempts to punish witnesses merely by processes of disclosure. The purpose of these decisions is clearly not that of giving aid to subversion but rather that of maintaining the integrity of the government and of constitutional rights, which are endangered not merely by subversive agents but by unrestricted activities of the government agencies themselves. The full import of these decisions remains yet to be determined.

76. Morton Grodzins, *The Loyal and the Disloyal* (1956).

77. See *ibid.*, p. 17.

78. United States v. Schwimmer, 279 U.S. 644, 648 (1929).

CHAPTER IV

1. For discussion, see Pendleton Herring, *The Impact of War* (1941).

2. For discussion, see Louis Smith, *American Democracy and Military Power* (1951).

3. *Code of Federal Regulations,* 1943 Supplement, Book 1, p. 43.

4. 88 *Congressional Record* 7044.

5. British *Parliamentary Debates,* 5th Series, Vol. 367, p. 26.

6. *Ibid.* For discussion of this subject in another context, see Carl Brent Swisher, "The Post-War Constitution," *Gaspar G. Bacon Lec-*

tures on the Constitution of the United States, 1940-1950 (1953), pp. 363-364. See also Edward S. Corwin, *Total War and the Constitution* (1947), pp. 62 ff.

7. See, for example, Yakus v. United States, 321 U.S. 414 (1944), Bowles v. Willingham, 321 U.S. 503 (1944), Lichter v. United States, 334 U.S. 742 (1948).
8. *Ex parte* Milligan, 4 Wallace 2, 109 (1866).
9. Quoted in the brief of David Dudley Field, *Ex parte* Milligan, 18 L. Ed. 285.
10. 4 Wallace 127.
11. *Ibid.*, p. 127.
12. *Ibid.*, p. 140.
13. *New York Times*, December 14, 1917.
14. Alpheus T. Mason, *Harlan Fiske Stone: Pillar of the Law* (1956), p. 648.
15. *Ibid.*, pp. 649-650. See especially his dissent in United States v. Pink, 315 U.S. 203, 242 (1942).
16. Proclamation No. 2561, July 2, 1942, 7 F.R. 5101.
17. July 2, 1942, 7 F.R. 5103.
18. Mason, *op. cit.*, p. 656.
19. 317 U.S. 1.
20. See Mason, *op. cit.*, pp. 664-666.
21. Quoted, Hirabayashi v. United States, 320 U.S. 81, 86 (1943).
22. For discussion, see Jacobus Ten Broeck *et al.*, *Japanese-American Evacuation and Resettlement* (1954), pp. 114-116.
23. 320 U.S. 93.
24. 323 U.S. 214.
25. *Ex parte* Endo, 323 U.S. 283 (1944).
26. *Ex parte* Merryman, Federal Cases No. 9487. For discussion, see Carl Brent Swisher, *American Constitutional Development* (2d ed., 1954), pp. 278-281.
27. Korematsu v. United States, 323 U.S. 214, 248 (1944).
28. *Ibid.*, p. 246.
29. See Ten Broeck, *op. cit.*, pp. 218-220.
30. 327 U.S. 304 (1946).
31. *Ibid.*, p. 324.
32. *Ibid.*, pp. 334-335.
33. *Ibid.*, p. 343.
34. 327 U.S. 1 (1946).
35. *Ibid.*, pp. 27-28.
36. *Ibid.*, p. 79.
37. Hirota v. MacArthur, 335 U.S. 876 (1948).
38. Hirota v. MacArthur, 338 U.S. 197 (1949).
39. For citations, see Hirota v. MacArthur, 335 U.S. 876, 877, note 1 (1948), and Johnson v. Eisentrager, 339 U.S. 763, 768, note 1 (1950).
40. 339 U.S. 763.
41. *Ibid.*, p. 776.
42. *Ibid.*, p. 797.

43. *Ibid.*, p. 798.
44. 64 Stat. 108.
45. Statement of Major General Thomas H. Green, Judge Advocate General of the Army, *Uniform Code of Military Justice*, Hearings, Sub-committee of the Senate Committee on Armed Services, 81st Cong., 1st Sess., on S 857 and HR 4080, p. 256.
46. *Ibid.*, p. 257.
47. United States *ex rel.* Toth v. Quarles, 350 U.S. 11, 21-22 (1955).
48. *Ibid.*, p. 44.
49. 140 U.S. 453.
50. Kinsella v. Krueger, 351 U.S. 470 (1956), Reid v. Covert, 351 U.S. 487 (1956).
51. Kinsella v. Krueger, 351 U.S. 470, 476-477 (1956).
52. Reid v. Covert, 1 L. Ed. 2d 92 (1956).
53. Quoted by Frederick Bernays Wiener, *Uniform Code of Military Justice, op. cit.*, p. 139.
54. Youngstown Sheet and Tube Co. v. Sawyer, 343 U.S. 579 (1952).

CHAPTER V

1. See, for example, New York v. Miln, 8 Peters 120 (1837), and Passenger Cases (Smith v. Turner and Norris v. Boston), 7 Howard 283 (1849).
2. People v. Downer, 7 Cal. 169 (1862).
3. See, for example, Barbier v. Connally, 113 U.S. 27 (1885), Soon Hing v. Crowley, 113 U.S. 703 (1885), Yick Wo v. Hopkins, 118 U.S. 356 (1886). For discussion of the Chinese problem, see Carl Brent Swisher, *Stephen J. Field: Craftsman of the Law* (1930), chap. viii.
4. Chae Chan Ping v. United States, 130 U.S. 581 (1889), Ekiu v. United States, 142 U.S. 651 (1892).
5. Fong Yue Ting v. United States, 149 U.S. 698 (1893).
6. Wong Wing v. United States, 163 U.S. 228 (1896). However, for development of the concept of administrative finality in determination of facts, in a case that perhaps more than incidentally involved a Chinese, see United States v. Ju Toy, 198 U.S. 253 (1905).
7. See Toyota v. United States, 268 U.S. 402, 408 (1925).
8. Terrace v. Thompson, 263 U.S. 197, 221 (1923).
9. Oyama v. California, 332 U.S. 633 (1948).

10. Takahashi v. Fish & Game Commission, 334 U.S. 410 (1948).
11. Rice v. Sioux City Cemetery, 349 U.S. 70 (1955).
12. The remainder of this chapter was published in approximately this form in the *Journal of Politics,* Vol. XIX (May, 1957), 167-183.
13. Vincent C. Hopkins, *Dred Scott's Case* (1951), p. 6.
14. Carl Brent Swisher, *Roger B. Taney* (1935), p. 491.
15. Dred Scott v. Sandford, 19 Howard 393, 407 (1857).
16. *Ibid.*, p. 404.
17. *Ibid.*, p. 450.
18. *Ibid.*, p. 426.
19. Swisher, *op. cit.*, p. 582.
20. Strader v. Graham, 5 Howard 215 (1851).
21. Texas v. White, 7 Wallace 700 (1869).
22. See, for example, Horace E. Flack, *Adoption of the Fourteenth Amendment* (1908); Benjamin B. Kendrick (ed.), *Journal of the Joint Committee of Fifteen on Reconstruction* (1914); Joseph B. James, *The Framing of the Fourteenth Amendment* (1956).
23. 16 Wallace 36.
24. United States v. Cruickshank, Federal Cases No. 14,897, p. 710 (1874).
25. See especially C. Vann Woodward, *Reunion and Reaction* (1951).
26. Civil Rights Cases, 109 U.S. 3, 25 (1883).
27. *Ibid.*, p. 26.
28. *Ibid.*, pp. 58-59.
29. Brown v. Board of Education, 347 U.S. 483, 495 (1954).
30. 305 U.S. 337.
31. *Ibid.*, p. 353.
32. 163 U.S. 537.
33. 332 U.S. 631.
34. 334 U.S. 1.
35. 339 U.S. 637.
36. 339 U.S. 629.
37. Brown v. Board of Education, 345 U.S. 972-973 (1953).
38. Brown v. Board of Education, 349 U.S. 294, 301 (1955).
39. Brown v. Board of Education, 347 U.S. 483, 492-493 (1954).
40. 347 U.S. 501.
41. 347 U.S. 495.
42. For indication in recent years of Supreme Court sentiments concerning the scope of the power of Congress to legislate on civil rights, see Screws v. United States, 325 U.S. 91 (1945). For discussion, see Julius Cohen, "The Screws Case: Federal Protection of Negro Rights," *Columbia Law Review,* Vol. XLVI (January, 1946), pp. 94-106.

CHAPTER VI

1. Benjamin N. Cardozo, *The Paradoxes of Legal Science* (1928), p. 2.
2. *Ex parte* Republic of Peru, 318 U.S. 578, 603 (1943). For a more recent statement by the same author, see Kinsella v. Krueger, 351 U.S. 470, 485 (1956), in which it is said that "Wisdom, like good wine, requires maturing."
3. Robert H. Jackson, *The Supreme Court in the American System of Government* (1955), p. 9.
4. Marbury v. Madison, 1 Cranch 137, 177 (1803).
5. Roscoe Pound, "Organization of Courts," *Journal of the American Judicature Society,* Vol. XI, p. 69.
6. See Jerome Frank, *Courts on Trial* (1950), chap. xviii.
7. McCulloch v. Maryland, 4 Wheaton 316, 407 (1819).
8. *Ibid.,* p. 431.
9. Charles River Bridge v. Warren Bridge, 11 Peters 420, 548 (1837).
10. Munn v. Illinois, 94 U.S. 113, 134 (1877).
11. Lochner v. New York, 198 U.S. 45, 76 (1905).
12. Panhandle Oil Co. v. Mississippi *ex rel.* Knox, 277 U.S. 218, 223 (1928).
13. New State Ice Co. v. Liebmann, 285 U.S. 262, 311 (1932).
14. Hebert v. Louisiana, 272 U.S. 312, 316-317 (1926).
15. Palko v. Connecticut, 302 U.S. 319, 325 (1937).
16. United States v. Butler, 297 U.S. 1, 62-63 (1936).
17. *Ibid.,* pp. 78-79.
18. *Ibid.,* p. 87.
19. *Ibid.*
20. West Coast Hotel Co. v. Parrish, 300 U.S. 379, 402 (1937).
21. Adamson v. California, 332 U.S. 46, 75 (1947).
22. *Ibid.,* p. 65.
23. American Federation of Labor v. American Sash and Door Co., 335 U.S. 538, 555 (1949).
24. *Ibid.,* p. 65.
25. Dennis v. United States, 341 U.S. 494, 508 (1951).
26. "Jurisprudence" in Margaret E. Hall (ed.), *Selected Writings of Benjamin Nathan Cardozo* (1947), p. 9.
27. American Federation of Labor v. American Sash and Door Co., 335 U.S. 538, 557 (1949).
28. Solesbee v. Balkcom, 339 U.S. 9, 16 (1950).

29. Oliver Wendell Holmes, Jr., "The Path of the Law," *Collected Legal Papers* (1920), p. 181.
30. In the Matter of the Indiana Transportation Co., 244 U.S. 456, 457 (1917).
31. For discussion, see Carl Brent Swisher, "The Supreme Court—Need for Reevaluation," *Virginia Law Review,* Vol. XL, pp. 837-851.
32. West Coast Hotel Co. v. Parrish, 300 U.S. 379 (1937).
33. National Labor Relations Board v. Jones & Laughlin Steel Co., 301 U.S. 1 (1937).
34. See Steward Machine Co. v. Davis, 301 U.S. 548 (1937), and Helvering v. Davis, 301 U.S. 619 (1937).
35. For portrayal and discussion of multiple alignments, see especially C. Herman Pritchett, *The Roosevelt Court* (1948).
36. See Samuel J. Konefsky, *The Legacy of Holmes and Brandeis* (1956).
37. Pound, *op. cit.,* p. 69.
38. Jackson, *op. cit.,* p. 16.
39. See Walter Lippmann, *The Public Philosophy* (1955).
40. Alpheus T. Mason, *Harlan Fiske Stone: Pillar of the Law* (1956), p. 513, note.
41. *Ibid.,* p. 365.
42. Jackson, *op. cit.,* pp. 20-21.

Index